*To Ami, who recognized what was in my heart
before I did. Thanks a million!*

*And to Jerry, for continuing to fight
the good fight. I love you.*

For as many as are the promises of God, in Him they are yes; therefore also through Him is our Amen to the glory of God through us.

2 Corinthians 1:20

Allison

This wasn't the life Allison Kavanagh had imagined for herself, but it was what her life had become. Like it or not, she had to get on with it.

She turned the key in the lock.

Hidden away in the mountains north of Boise, the two-story log house—built many decades before but completely remodeled on the inside—was open and airy with a state-of-the-art kitchen, modern efficiencies throughout, and spectacular views of the rugged Idaho mountains from every window. The place had been left to Allison four years earlier in her great-aunt's will. Never in her wildest dreams had Allison imagined she would end up living in it one day. Perhaps Aunt Emma had seen the future a little more clearly than she had.

Welcome to your new home.

A lump formed in her throat, but she fought back the tears. She was weary of crying—it was all she'd done for months and months. Sometimes it felt like years and years. Setting her mouth, she dropped her purse onto the small table inside the front door.

Some of her own furniture filled the living room. She was glad of it. Made the place feel a little less foreign to her. Not that it *was* foreign to her. She'd visited her aunt's home many times throughout her life, and after it had come into Allison's possession, it had served as an occasional getaway, a place of peace when life's storms became too much to handle.

Dear Aunt Emma. The sister of Allison's maternal grandmother, Emma Carter had been considered somewhat of a "rebel" in the family. Never married and financially independent because of her success as a nature photographer, added to sound investments and careful spending, she'd lived as she pleased. Oh, the stories Aunt Emma used to tell about World Wars I and II, the Roaring Twenties, the Great Depression. If ever a woman was born with the gift of storytelling, it had been Emma Carter. No wonder Allison had adored her.

"How do I get on with my life, Aunt Emma?" she whispered.

If Aunt Emma were still alive, she would have answered honestly and directly. No mincing words. Emma Carter had never sugarcoated anything for anybody. Not even for her favorite—as she'd always called Allison—and only—as Allison had pointed out in return—great niece. But Aunt Emma was gone. Allison would have to find the answers on her own or muddle along as best she could without them.

She passed through the living room and walked down the short hallway to the master bedroom. The new queen-sized four-poster she'd purchased sat against the opposite wall, bare of bedclothes other than a quilted mattress cover. Staring at the bed, she felt her aloneness afresh. It burned through her like salt in an open wound.

She looked away.

In a corner of the bedroom sat her large desk and credenza. It too was naked. Allison hadn't entrusted her MacBook, large external display, or printer to the movers. Those important items were still in her car in the driveway.

A design deadline loomed closer. She'd best get her office set up and make certain the Internet was turned on as promised by the cable provider. Her to-do list was too long to ignore, even for a few days. And besides, keeping busy took her mind off many less pleasant realities. Immersing herself in work had been her salvation. For years, really, but especially over the past eleven months. Ever since the day she'd uttered her ultimatum.

The lump in her throat returned. She swallowed again.

"Tough love" some would have called her take-it-or-leave-it demand, and she'd been certain tough love was required in the situation. But she'd believed what she said would be that last straw, that illusive bottom, those words that would change everything.

They *had* changed everything. Just not the way she'd hoped they would. Not the way she'd wanted. Not for the better. Not as promised.

Why didn't You keep Your promise?

It was the most she'd said to God in a while. The ability to pray seemed to have shriveled inside of her. One more loss added to so many others.

With a shake of her head, Allison retraced her footsteps to the living room, went out onto the wide redwood deck that circled three sides of the house, and descended the steps to her pale gold SUV parked in the driveway. From behind the driver's seat she released her dog from his crate and set him on the ground. Gizmo sniffed at his new surroundings.

"You stay close. I don't want an eagle or a bear having you for lunch." The tricolored papillon perked up his ears, and she couldn't keep from smiling. "You're such a good boy."

She'd bought Gizmo from a local breeder to help fill the vast emptiness that had surrounded her after her husband walked out the door, leaving her and her ultimatum in the dust. Having an active puppy around had helped ease the emptiness too. There was always something she needed to do for the little guy—feed him, take him for a walk, give him a bath, let him out to do his business.

She'd read somewhere that owning a papillon meant never going to the bathroom alone, and it was true. Gizmo followed her everywhere. He slept on the unused right side of the bed. He sat near her feet when she ate, a hopeful expression on his face even though she never let him eat table scraps. He curled up beside her on the sofa while she watched television. He lay in his dog bed under her desk when she was on the computer. He was her constant and best companion, and she loved him for making her feel less alone.

Perhaps she would become that crazy old lady who lived in a log cabin in the mountains, talking only to her dog. Or dogs. She could get Gizmo a friend or two. Or maybe she should acquire a half-dozen cats. She could give herself a funky haircut and let it go all frizzy and kinky. She could dress in bright, baggy clothes. But then, who would know if she was crazy or not? Who would see her? A dense forest separated her from her nearest neighbors, and she was miles up a winding highway to the nearest town. Not to mention that her only child, Meredith, lived halfway across the country.

A crazy old lady. She closed her eyes and released a sigh. Forty-five wasn't old, but some days it seemed like it. Some days forty-five felt like ninety.

She went to the back of the Tribeca and opened the rear door. Her LED computer display was in its original box with a handle. She grabbed it along with her laptop case and headed into the house. And for the next several hours, while she hooked up electronics in the bedroom and the living room and otherwise settled in, she managed to keep her thoughts from returning to the sad place they too often traveled to.

That was no small victory.

Allison

It was the silence that awakened her the next morning. She'd forgotten how quiet the forest could be, especially in the spring before vacationers found their way to the campgrounds that dotted the area and in the fall when the hunters were out in force. In Boise the sun would already be full up. Here, it took longer before it topped the eastern ridge. But there was still enough light in the room to see Gizmo staring at her, silently asking to be let out.

"All right," she grumbled. "All right. I'm getting up."

Gizmo barked and jumped off the bed.

Allison reached for her robe as she sat up. It might be May on the calendar, but there was a wintery chill in the morning air.

"I need coffee," she whispered as she headed toward the front door.

She stood on the deck, hugging herself to keep warm while she kept an eye on Gizmo. When he returned, they went straight to the kitchen. She grabbed her favorite mug, plopped a K-Cup into her Cuisinart coffeemaker, and pressed Brew. When her coffee was ready, she carried the mug into the living room and settled onto her favorite chair. Watching sunlight kiss the tops of tall trees, she let her thoughts meander through time, at last settling on her parents.

Robert and Margaret Knight. Bob and Maggie to their close friends. If ever two people loved each other, it was her mom and dad. Growing up, when her dad's car pulled into the driveway at 5:40 p.m. each weekday, her mom's eyes lit up. She acted as though she hadn't seen him in nine days instead of nine hours. Dad was the same way with her.

Allison and her brother, Chuck, had golden childhoods. They truly did. They were loved and encouraged and supported. They had everything they needed and plenty of what they wanted. Their mom had hauled them all over creation for their various activities—ballet, football, piano, track, Brownies, Cub Scouts—and she'd beamed with pride over their accomplishments. And their dad had been the rock at the center of their home. He still was.

Allison's extended family had never been huge, but all of them—"in-laws and outlaws," her dad used to call them—were close. They used to gather together for birthdays and Thanksgiving and Christmas and Easter. They used to have summer barbecues and weekend card parties. They'd gone camping together, the whole lot of them, sometimes in the forest behind Aunt Emma's log house.

Good food and lots of laughter. Those had been two constants throughout Allison's growing up years. Foolishly, she'd thought that was how it was in every family. Naively, she'd thought that was how it would be after she married Tony and they had a family of their own.

It hadn't turned out quite that way.

Tony Kavanagh. Star quarterback and president of the high school debate team. Straight-A student all the way through his schooling. Tall, dark, and handsome. A walking cliché. Whatever he'd touched in those early years had turned to gold. She'd loved him almost from the first moment she laid eyes on him as he walked across the Boise State campus.

Did she love him still? No. Although she still loved the

memories of the good times they'd had as a family. Mostly, what she felt now was grief. The dream of a happy, lasting marriage had died a slow and painful death, and she'd buried it and mourned it. Mourned it even now.

She gave her head a shake, hoping to dislodge the sad thoughts. She should get off her fanny and get to work. She had a website design to finish by the end of next week. The client had been patient, understanding when Allison needed an extra few weeks because of her move. But she didn't want to miss the new deadline. She prided herself on being on time.

And yet, even knowing this, when she rose from the chair, she didn't head for her desk, nor did she walk to the bathroom so she could shower and dress. Instead, after brewing a second cup of coffee, she wandered up the stairs. She looked into the two bedrooms, empty except for boxes she needed to go through again and the treadmill she hadn't used in weeks. She'd given away and donated many possessions before the move, but there was still so much *stuff*. How had she accumulated it all? How had *they* accumulated it all? She needed to get rid of even more.

But not today. I don't want to go through it today.

She sighed and was about to retrace her steps but stopped when she noticed the trapdoor that led to the attic. Aunt Emma hadn't allowed Allison and Chuck to go up there when they were children. Allison had never asked to do so as an adult. And it hadn't occurred to her to explore the attic after the house came into her possession. To be honest, she'd forgotten it was even accessible via the door in the hall ceiling. She hadn't looked up until now.

Had Aunt Emma kept anything in the attic? Had she emptied it before her death?

A short rope was strung from a handle, the opposite end looped around a hook screwed into the wall. Allison unwound the loop, took a breath, and pulled downward. The trapdoor opened with surprising ease and the wooden ladder slid to the floor. As she put her foot on the bottom rung, she halfway expected to hear Aunt Emma scold her from downstairs.

"Wait here, Gizmo."

Her dog lay down, resting his muzzle on his paws.

When Allison's head rose above the insulated opening, she discovered morning light streaming through windows on both the front and back ends of the attic room. A naked lightbulb hanging from the ceiling told her the room was wired for electricity should she ever want to be up here at night. She doubted that would happen, but a brief glance around located the light switch.

There were numerous cardboard boxes stacked at one end of the room. A dress form stood guard near one window, a measuring tape draped around its neck. Beside the dress form was an old treadle sewing machine. When Allison was a little girl, both of those items were in Aunt Emma's bedroom, where Allison's desk sat now. It must have been a good twenty-five years since she'd last seen them.

She climbed the rest of the way up the ladder and stood in the center of the attic. To her left, against the sloped sides of the attic, were two battered steamer trunks and one cedar hope chest. Instinct told her the cardboard boxes would hold "things" while the trunks and chest would hold keepsakes. She was drawn in the latter's direction.

Emma

The United States declared war on Germany on Emma Isobel Carter's tenth birthday—April 6, 1917. Forever after, even when she was older and knew better, Emma would have the strange feeling she'd been the cause of one of her family's greatest sadnesses. But on that particular birthday, all she knew was that the adults wore grim expressions and her birthday party, complete with cake and ice cream, felt sad.

Although Emma had hoped for books for her tenth birthday, the gift from her parents was a doll, identical to the one her sister, Elizabeth, had received on her ninth birthday two months earlier. Emma didn't play with dolls, but Mama never seemed to notice. Emma would much rather tuck herself in a corner somewhere and read a book about foreign places. Or climb a tree. Or skip rocks on the pond. Or ride her horse bareback in the pasture.

Emma knew, even at her tender age, she would never be as pretty as her sister. Elizabeth—younger by ten months—was more than pretty. She was beautiful. Everyone said so. Liza, as Emma called her sister, had golden ringlets and sky-blue eyes and a smile that melted hearts, Emma's included. Liza was sweet and charming without even trying; it came as natural to her as drawing breath.

That night, well after Liza had fallen asleep, Emma got out of bed and went downstairs to get a drink of water. That was when she overheard her parents talking in the parlor.

"Will you have to go, Roger?"

"I don't believe so. Not unless the war drags on."

"It's already dragged on. England's been fighting in Europe for years. So many men have died and still it goes on."

"Don't worry, Pearl. They'll call up unmarried men first. Younger men. I don't think I'll have to go."

"But my brother will. Won't he?"

"Yes, Stewart would be called up. If there's a conscription, they'll take the younger and single men first. But I imagine he'll volunteer before that could happen."

Her mother's voice fell to a whisper. "You don't really think he'll volunteer, do you?"

"I think he might, Pearl. Young men always seem eager to rush off to war, and your brother has a strong sense of patriotism."

Her mother started to cry.

Emma returned to her bedroom without getting a glass of water from the kitchen. She'd lost her thirst. She didn't understand everything her parents had said, but she understood Uncle Stewart was probably going away. Her uncle was the one adult who seemed to like Emma just the way she was, and now he would be leaving.

She stood at the window, looking out at the moonless night. A tomboy—that's what Mama called Emma sometimes—and she didn't make it sound like a good thing to be. But one time, when he'd heard what Mama said, Uncle Stewart winked at Emma and whispered, "You go right ahead and be a tomboy. Climb those trees. Ride those horses. Read all those books. Go as high as you can as fast as you can and learn as much as you can."

When she heard Uncle Stewart's voice saying those things

in her head, she wasn't afraid to do anything, try anything, be anything. But when she couldn't hear his voice, when he wasn't around to encourage her with a grin and a wink, it was easier to just do what others, like Mama and Liza, wanted her to do and to be what they wanted her to be.

Emma turned away from the window, crawled into bed, and buried her face in her pillow. Then, like her mother, she cried.

Allison

Allison opened Aunt Emma's hope chest first. It was filled to the absolute brim. At the very top was a layer of old newspapers, and peeking out from one corner was a small glass horse, silver in color. She picked it up and held it in the palm of her hand.

Allison had always found it interesting, the things people held on to. Perhaps more so because—despite the number of boxes in the second-floor bedrooms—she wasn't much of a saver. She hadn't kept much memorabilia from Meredith's childhood, and the important items Allison had saved, she'd given to her daughter when Meredith had taken a job transfer to Texas.

Did that make her a bad mother? She'd pondered the question more than once over the years. But she didn't like clutter. She didn't want to be afraid to open closet doors worried about being hit in the head with tumbling keepsakes. She disliked drawers that were hard to close because they were too full. She hated the idea of a garage—or spare bedrooms—filled with boxes of *stuff* she would never look at again, unless she moved and was forced to see what was inside. And so she'd tossed and given away throughout her life. Whenever she purchased something new, she tried to get rid of something old. That rule had served her well.

Her mother, on the other hand, could have produced an array of Allison's childhood outfits in various sizes, all of her ballet costumes, all of her report cards, and any notes her teachers had sent home, from kindergarten through her senior year of high school. Heaven knew where her mother kept it all, especially after her parents sold their big house in Boise and retired to Phoenix.

Allison felt a sudden sting of missing Mom, Dad, and Meredith. Everyone she loved had moved away from her. Even Tony, although he hadn't gone as far as the others. He'd left her, not Idaho.

That thought made the missing worse.

Stop it.

She shook her head, refusing to give in to melancholy again. Not today. She would be strong for today. One day at a time. Like the practice of any good codependent in recovery. One day at a time. She could get through one day without sad thoughts, and if not one day, at least she could get through the next hour.

She closed the lid of the hope chest, deciding to go through it later. Maybe as a treat for getting her design work done each day. Because while she didn't save much herself, she was interested to see what Aunt Emma had thought worth keeping.

But it would have to wait. There was work to do.

She left the glass figurine on her desk then went down to the ground floor where she took a quick shower and, afterward, dressed in a pair of exercise Capri's and an oversized T-shirt—her favorite stay-at-home attire and one of the perks of being self-employed. She swept her dark hair into a ponytail and ignored makeup altogether. Who would see her? She didn't have any video chats scheduled, and her nearest neighbors probably didn't know she'd moved in, tucked back into the forest as her new home was.

After making herself another large cup of coffee, she turned on her computer, opened her current project, and set to work. When she looked up next, more than two hours had passed. Her lower back complained, as if to prove the point. She rose from her chair and stretched.

If she was smart, she would plug in the treadmill and put a

few miles on it. But why walk on a machine when the mountains were waiting outside her door?

She slipped her arms into the sleeves of a bulky-knit sweater that reached to her thighs, put on her athletic shoes, and headed outdoors with Gizmo on a leash. They didn't stop moving until they reached the end of the long driveway. There, she took a deep breath of the fresh pine-scented air. Glorious! She should have done this yesterday. She would try to do it daily from now on, at least in the warmer months. She would make a walk through the forest or along the river a part of her routine. She would explore every trail she could find. She would walk fast and breathe deeply and lose fifteen unwanted pounds. She would improve her outlook on life. She would stop feeling sorry for herself, even if just for brief periods of time. Maybe she would even learn to talk to God again.

Allison and Gizmo crossed the highway and descended to the riverbank.

Learn to talk to God again. How sad that she'd forgotten how to pray. No, she hadn't forgotten how. She'd simply stopped doing it—and not intentionally. It just . . . happened. Perhaps because she'd stopped believing prayer made any difference. She didn't want to feel that way. It didn't mean she'd stopped believing in God or had turned her back on Jesus or didn't trust in her salvation.

Was she angry with God? Perhaps. She'd been so sure He'd made a promise to her, a promise that had gone unfulfilled. She'd counted on it. Believed in it. Tried to do everything she thought necessary on her part in order to realize the promise. But it never happened. And since God didn't lie it meant she'd heard wrong. It meant she didn't know His voice the way she'd once thought she did.

"So even if I prayed now, how would I know if You answered?"

Emma

1918

Emma's uncle Stewart never came home from the Great War. He died in the summer of 1918 during the Second Battle of the Marne outside of Paris. When the news of his death arrived, the Carter household went into deep mourning, Emma's mother inconsolable over the loss of her younger brother.

No one seemed to notice Emma was heartbroken too. She was, after all, only a child. What could she understand of death? But she understood more than the grown-ups knew.

To find solace, she took long walks in the foothills above the Carter home. That was the summer when Emma learned to talk to God. Not just to say her prayers the way she did each night, on her knees beside her bed, hands steepled in front of her eyes, with her mother or father observing from the doorway. No, this was different. So different, she wondered if the minister at church would approve. Her mother wouldn't condone it. Emma was convinced of that.

But God knew what she thought and felt already. And if He already knew, she might as well speak her mind out loud. So she let the pain pour out, beginning with asking God why He hadn't protected Uncle Stewart the way she'd asked Him to in her prayers. Faithful prayers. Daily prayers. Fervent prayers. From the time Uncle Stewart joined the army, Emma had prayed for his safe return every single day. Had God said no to her request or hadn't He heard her pleas for safety?

She'd loved her uncle more than anybody else in the world. More than her mother and father. More than her sister. Sometimes Emma had pretended he was the Prince Charming of fairy tales, and when she grew up, he would ride in on his white horse and carry her off to a castle on a high hill. A silly thing to pretend, but it made her happy all the same.

But that would never happen now. Because she would never see Uncle Stewart again.

Allison

Allison's and Gizmo's first week in their new home passed quickly. Allison's work kept her busy during the daytime hours, and in the evenings and on the weekend, she slowly perused keepsakes from the first of Aunt Emma's trunks—some jewelry, an envelope of tax receipts for this house and land from the early 1930s, two ancient 35mm cameras, a large collection of loose black-and-white photographs, some that were wrinkled and worn, clipped newspaper articles and obituaries, a bundle of letters.

Allison had never had the time nor the inclination to delve deeply into her family's history. She'd been satisfied with the stories she knew and with her own memories. But as she looked through the photographs Aunt Emma had kept—not the nature photos that had brought her fame but the ones of people—curiosity began to grow. She recognized a few faces here and there, but the majority of them were strangers to her. There was one man in particular who seemed to have been a favorite in Aunt Emma's early years. There were photographs of him alone as well as with other people about his own age and a few of him with Aunt Emma, one with his arm around her shoulders.

Had any of these photographs been Aunt Emma's early efforts with a camera? Allison didn't think so. They seemed so . . . different—yet certainly intriguing. She'd never imagined Aunt Emma with a boyfriend. Emma Carter hadn't been unattractive, by any means, but neither had she been a beauty like

Allison's grandmother, Elizabeth Carter Hendricks. Allison's assumption about a lack of suitors was because her spinster aunt—what a horrid term that was—had never mentioned having a sweetheart. Never. But judging by these photographs, Allison's assumption had been wrong.

Perhaps her mother could tell her who the man in the pictures was. Allison reached for the telephone to call her, but a knock on the door—the sound making her and Gizmo jump in surprise—stopped her from punching the Phoenix number. Gizmo barked as he hopped up and down in front of the door.

"Gizmo, sit. Be still." She stood and, as she did so, quickly checked her appearance in the mirror she'd hung last week to the left of the door. She looked presentable enough to see who'd come calling.

The knock sounded again.

"Coming." She moved to the door and pulled it open.

And there stood Tony. Her heart skittered. She hadn't seen him since before the divorce became final, and it surprised her to see him now.

"Hello, Allie."

No one else called her that. Only him. She used to love it. Now, not so much.

"Hello, Tony. I didn't expect to see you." Her eyes narrowed as she studied him. Looking. Wondering. Suspecting. Hating. Fearing.

Old habits died hard. Especially when it came to Tony.

"May I come in?" he asked.

She took a step back. "Sure." She pushed the door wide open.

"Hey, mutt," he said to Gizmo.

Allison closed the door and released the dog from his sit. "Free."

"Wow." Tony moved into the center of the living room. "The

place looks really different from the last time I was up here. I like what you've done with it."

She motioned for him to sit in one of the chairs. "Can I get you something to drink? I've got some diet soda or I could make you a cup of coffee."

He waved the offer away. "No, thanks. I'm not thirsty." Rather than sitting, he moved to the fireplace and looked at several framed photographs of Meredith and Aunt Emma and Allison's parents.

Strange, the way his presence unsettled her. It shouldn't. She knew Tony better than any other person in the world. True, she didn't love him anymore. He'd killed her love. Killed it by degrees. So what was it she felt for him now? She couldn't say.

"What do you want, Tony?" The question sounded harsh. She supposed she'd meant it to.

He faced her and shrugged. "Just to know how you're getting along."

As if you care.

"I'd like us to be friends, Allie."

Friends. Really? He drove all the way up here to say he wanted them to be friends? She had a sudden and terrible urge to throw something at him. To hurt him. To make him rue the day he'd met her, the same way she rued it.

"Have you heard from Meredith?" Tony raked the fingers of his right hand through his hair. "She hasn't returned any of my phone calls lately."

Anger drained from Allison as quickly as it had burst to life. She sank onto the sofa. "She's doing well. Loves her job. Making new friends. She's busy."

"You'd think she'd want to talk to her old man once in a while."

"Give her time. She's still upset over the divorce."

"But she talks to you."

I'm not the one who walked out. I'm not the reason we're divorced. I'm not the one who—

"Things aren't going well at work." Tony finally sat. "Nothing I do seems to make the boss happy."

She was tempted to ask him how many times he'd shown up late for work. How many times had he called in sick? But she managed to swallow the questions. She couldn't control him. She couldn't fix him. She had to let go.

Let go.

The words reverberated in Allison's chest. As if it were only yesterday, she remembered where she'd been and what she'd been doing the first time she heard those words in her heart. God's quiet, familiar voice, but the command so clear, so unwelcome. She'd held on to Tony and their marriage tightly for a long, long time. God had promised her a different outcome. How could He tell her to let go? Why had He done that instead of giving her the miracle she'd prayed for?

She stood. "I've got to get to work, Tony. I'm sorry. Maybe you should call next time before you drive all this way. You've got the number. I didn't change it. Cell service isn't good here, but the house number always works."

It occurred to her as he rose from the chair that he looked tired. Dark circles ringed his eyes. He'd aged over the past year. His hair, which needed a trim, had more gray in it. Come to think of it, he looked more than tired. He looked sad, beaten even. She was tempted to change her mind, to invite him to stay, perhaps offer him a meal. She resisted the temptation.

"Yeah, I've got the number." Tony moved toward the door. As he pulled it open, he said, "Sorry to take too much of your time . . ." He met her gaze. "Take care of yourself, Allie."

"You too."

He glanced back at her, offered a tight smile, then went out, closing the door behind him.

He didn't leave her thoughts quite that quickly.

Spring 1987

On their fourth date, after a lovely dinner at a favorite steak-house, Tony drove up 8th Street into the foothills on Boise's north boundary. He parked the truck on a rise where they could watch the full moon rise over the eastern mountains. After a few minutes of silence, he put his arm around her shoulders and drew her close to his side.

Her heart hammered, the way it always did when he held her. Could he hear it? Could he feel her pulse shaking the pickup?

"There it comes," he said. "I can't get over how big the moon looks on a night like this. Especially up here."

Allison made a sound of agreement in her throat.

Tony looked at her then. "You know what you've done, Allie Knight?"

"What?"

"You've made me fall in love with you."

She held her breath, amazed by what she'd heard. Afraid she was imagining it. Slowly, he brought his lips to hers. A million butterflies were loosed in her stomach.

When he drew back, he whispered, "Do you think you might learn to love me too?"

"Oh, Tony. I already do."

He grinned. "You do? Why didn't you say so before this?"

Because I was afraid you wouldn't ever say you love me. Because even if you did, I didn't want to be the first to say it.

"Marry me?" His voice was low. It poured over her like honey, golden and warm.

Now she *knew* she was imagining things.

"Say you'll marry me, Allie. Next year, after you graduate, let's get married. I should have a good job by then and be able to support us. My folks like you and your folks like me. Even your brother likes me."

Why be sensible? Let's elope. Let's elope tonight.

He kissed her again. With so much tenderness it brought tears to her eyes. How could anybody feel this happy and not explode from it?

Every fairy tale in the world had just come true for her.

Allison

The town of Kings Meadow, population 2,893, was up the narrow, winding highway several miles from Allison's home. Like many similar communities in Idaho, it had a fast-food joint, a restaurant that specialized in fried foods, two banks, three churches, and a public library. There was a mercantile, a gas station, a medical clinic, and the schools—classrooms for kindergarten through twelfth-grade students housed on a single campus, although in two different buildings, K through eighth grade in one, senior high in the other.

The residents of Kings Meadow and the surrounding mountains were a hardy, independent lot. They expected to see to their own needs, and usually they did. They were the sort who drove pickup trucks with rifle racks in the rear window and dogs in the truck bed. Men and women alike. Emma Carter had fit right in.

As Allison parked her Subaru in the lot of The Merc, she wondered if she would ever feel as if she belonged in that same way. She was and had always been a city girl. Boise wasn't New York or Seattle or LA, but it was plenty big enough. It had everything it needed to make it a great place to live—safe neighborhoods, a Shakespearean festival, a ballet company, a performing arts center, beautiful parks, a large university with a winning football team, a busy airport, easy access to the great outdoors, and much more. By comparison, Kings Meadow was a mere wide spot in the road.

"Be good," she told Gizmo as she freed him from his special doggie seat belt. Then she cracked the windows and got out of the car.

Inside the store Allison pushed a cart up and down the narrow grocery aisles. The choices were severely limited compared to the super stores down in the valley, but she wouldn't have to go hungry. And she would learn to do Costco runs, as Aunt Emma had called them, filling the back of her SUV with non-perishable bulk items.

"Excuse me," a woman said, breaking into Allison's thoughts. "Are you Emma Carter's niece?"

She met the other shopper's gaze. "Yes, I am."

"I'm Susan Lyle." Smiling, the woman held out her hand. "I've seen you in town before, but we've never been introduced."

Allison took the proffered hand. "Allison Kavanagh. It's nice to meet you."

Susan Lyle was perhaps sixty years old, give or take a few years. She had stone gray hair and a round face with smooth skin, except where smile lines had formed at the outer corners of her dark brown eyes. "The grapevine says you've moved into your aunt's place permanently."

"The grapevine would be correct."

"I'm glad. It's made me sad, having that house empty for so long. It was such a hive of activity when your aunt was alive. Emma Carter had the gift of hospitality like no one else I know. I don't believe she ever met a stranger."

Allison smiled, warmed by the comments.

"She was the first person to come welcome my husband and me when we moved here from LA. Many years ago now."

"Los Angeles? That must have been a bit of culture shock."

Susan laughed. "You have no idea. But we've loved living in Kings Meadow. It's one of the best decisions we ever made."

"What brought you to Idaho?"

"It was Ned's idea. Ned's my husband. He came up here on a hunting trip with his dad when he was a teenager, and he never forgot it. I was young and in love, enough that I'd go anywhere with him. So up to Idaho we came." Susan shook her head, laughing softly again. "Goodness. Listen to me. You must have better things to do than stand jawing with me in the grocery store."

Actually, Allison was loving the opportunity to hear another person talk. Gizmo was good company but not much of a conversationalist.

Susan continued, "I'd like to have you join me for coffee one morning so we could get better acquainted. I feel like I know you a little because of your aunt. Emma loved to brag on you and your brother. Here, this has my phone number and e-mail address on it." She held out a card. "Please give me a call soon."

"Thank you. I will. It was nice meeting you."

With a parting smile and a wave of her hand, Susan pushed her cart down the aisle.

Allison glanced at the card. She would call Susan Lyle, and she would call her soon. It would be nice to have a friend who wasn't an hour's drive away.

Emma

1922

Emma was fifteen the first time she laid eyes on Alexander James Monroe. Prohibition was the law of the land in 1922, but Alexander turned up at the Hudsucker party with a flask of liquor tucked in his pocket. It was supposed to be a big secret, but all of the kids knew he had it. Only the adults were kept in ignorance.

From where she sat in a corner of the parlor, Emma observed the goings-on. She hadn't wanted to come to this party, but Liza had begged and pleaded. Their parents wouldn't let fourteen-year-old Liza attend without Emma, and so, like it or not, Emma had to come. As if she could control what her self-assured, winsome younger sister got it into her head to do.

At the moment, Liza was making eyes at Alexander Monroe, and he, of course, was taking note of her. That was how boys were around Liza. They always noticed her. They couldn't help it. And Liza knew the power she wielded with males of almost every age. With a single flirtatious glance, she could make them do whatever she wanted.

But Emma also knew Alexander's reputation. At eighteen, he'd already broken at least as many girls' hearts as were represented in this house tonight. She didn't want her sister to be added to the collection. For all her flirtatious nature, Liza was still an innocent.

Better for it to be my heart at risk than hers. A foolish thought. Alexander Monroe wouldn't notice her. Most boys didn't.

Emma rose to her feet and moved around the edge of teenagers who were dancing the foxtrot. Envy made her chest tighten. Although she didn't want to admit it, she longed for a boy to ask her to dance. She would love to turn and glide her way around the parlor. She'd practiced in her bedroom lots of times.

But no boy asked Emma to dance. She was not the pretty sister. Liza was the beauty. By comparison, Emma faded into the wallpaper.

Just once, wouldn't it be nice to have a boy notice *her?* Wouldn't it be nice for Alexander Monroe to notice her? She didn't care about his reputation. He couldn't help it he was so good-looking that all the girls fell for him. He made Emma's heart race too, and she didn't even know him.

Yet. She didn't know him yet.

Allison

Allison was still in bed on Saturday morning when the phone rang. She answered with a groggy, "Hello?"

"Allison, dear. How are you?"

"Fine, Mom." She glanced at the digital clock on the night-stand. Not quite seven thirty. Her mother always had been an early bird.

"You don't sound fine. I hope you're not catching a cold. Moving can put such a strain on one's immune system. It weakens the body and opens you up to all sorts of germs."

Allison shifted the mouthpiece and cleared her throat. "I'm not sick. Honest. How's Dad?"

"He's fine. He left for the golf course half an hour ago. Told me to send his love and to say he'll call you later."

"Dad loves his golf."

"You like to golf. You should come down and go golfing with your father."

"I don't know when I'll find the time to do that. I've got so much work to do, and with the divorce and the move, I'm playing catch-up."

"Allison, I do wish you weren't all alone in those mountains. I worry about you so."

"I'm perfectly all right, Mom. If it makes you feel any better, I had a security system installed before I moved in. Not that security is much of an issue up here. I'll bet most residents leave their doors unlocked."

"Well, don't do that."

"I won't."

"I wish you would move down to Phoenix and stay with us. We have a lovely guest room that could be yours if you want it."

Forty-five and living with her parents again. Allison didn't think so. But she understood. If Meredith needed her, Allison would invite her to move in, in a heartbeat. That's what mothers did. They worried about their children no matter how old they got. They tried to make things better.

"If you came to live with us, Allison, you might meet a wonderful man. There are quite a few eligible widowers right here in our retirement community."

Allison didn't know if she should laugh or cry at the suggestion. She wasn't in the market for a new husband, especially not one old enough to retire.

As if reading her mind, her mother continued, "And they're not all your father's age either, so don't think that."

"I love you, Mom. I really and truly do. But I'm not looking for romance. Not with anybody."

"Are you still hoping Tony will—"

"Don't, Mom. I don't want to talk about Tony."

"But—"

"Don't."

"I'm still praying for him. I hope that's all right."

"Of course. He needs all the prayers he can get."

"I'm praying for you too."

Tears welled in Allison's eyes. "Thanks," she whispered, her throat suddenly tight.

"Well, tell me how you're settling in. Are you seeing lots of wildlife? Is there still snow on the ground?"

"No more snow." She pushed herself upright in the bed and leaned against the headboard, glad for the change of topics. "I saw some deer earlier in the week. And on my walks I've seen an eagle flying above the river a few times."

"One of my favorite photographs of Aunt Emma's was of an eagle flying through the canyon above the river. It still hangs in our living room."

"I know which one you mean. It must have been a favorite of hers too. It's among the ones she hung on the walls in the bedroom." Allison's gaze moved to the opposite wall. "They're still in here. I love them."

"You can see how much Emma loved those mountains. They're in almost every photograph she took."

"Hey, speaking of Aunt Emma and photos, she left some boxes and trunks in the attic. I've been going through things in my spare time, and there are quite a few photographs of some man I've never seen before. A few of her in the photo with him. They look like they were a couple. Do you know who he might have been?"

"A man? I haven't a clue. How old was she in the pictures?"

"Young. In her twenties, I suppose. Early twenties."

"That was before my time. I never heard her or Mother mention a love interest. I would remember if either one of them had. But those two could both be tight-lipped about some things."

Allison nodded in agreement. "You know what else was in one of the trunks? A wedding dress."

"A wedding dress?"

"Yes. Nothing fancy or expensive. Nothing like Grandma Elizabeth's. Whose dress do you suppose it was?"

"I haven't a clue."

"Made me wonder if Aunt Emma was engaged at one time and then the romance went south."

Her mother laughed softly. "That would be quite the secret for Emma and Mother to keep all of those years. Can't imagine why they would. The dress must have belonged to a friend or a distant cousin or something."

Gizmo chose that moment to jump off the bed and whine.

"Listen, Mom. I've got to go. The dog's begging to be let out. If you want, I can call you back when he's through."

"No. I don't suppose that's necessary. But do call me in a few days."

"Okay, I'll do that. I love you, Mom."

"I love you too, dear. And remember, I'm praying for you."

"I'll remember. Give my love to Dad."

They both said good-bye, and Allison put the portable handset into the charger. She was tempted to nestle back under the covers, but Gizmo let her know he was growing impatient. She got out of bed, pulled on her bathrobe, and escorted the dog outside.

Standing on the deck while keeping an eye on Gizmo, Allison drew in a deep breath. After ten days, she felt mostly settled in, like she belonged here. It surprised her a little, how fast that had happened. She'd expected to feel as if she were visiting her vacation home for quite some time.

She and Tony had lived in their house on Mountain View Drive for more than twenty years. Meredith had grown up there. How many improvements had they made to the place? Dozens. And each one of those improvements had helped make the home uniquely theirs. If she closed her eyes, she could smell cookies baking in the oven or picture Tony standing at the gas grill on the patio or see the family sitting near the Christmas tree, Meredith opening presents. Memories. Good memories. There were many of them.

But Tony lived in that house alone now. Allison hadn't tried to fight him for it. Her lawyer had counseled her to sell the house and divide the proceeds, but she hadn't been able to follow that advice. She was still trying to rescue him, she supposed. But the mortgage was paid off, and she wouldn't have to worry that he had no place to live if things got bad for him again.

And things always got bad again for Tony.

Summer 1988

Allison and Tony had been married not quite three months when she discovered she was pregnant. Having a baby so soon hadn't been in the plans, but Allison wasn't sorry. She loved Tony so much. Having his child would simply make their marriage all the happier.

It was the Saturday of Labor Day weekend when they drove over to Tony's parents' home for a barbecue. It was the perfect opportunity to share the news with both families, since everyone would be there.

Dad Kavanagh had just slapped the steaks on the grill when Tony clanked a fork against his glass. "Hey, everyone. I've got something I need to tell you." He looked through the screened door to the kitchen at their two mothers. "Mom, can you and Maggie come join us?"

"Of course, dear."

Tony motioned for Allison to come stand beside him, which she did, making sure not to look anyone in the eyes for fear she would give away their secret too soon.

Once both their mothers had come out to the patio, joining Tony's and Allison's fathers and her brother, Chuck, Tony put his arm around Allison's back. "Allie and I have important news." He leaned over and kissed her on the temple. "We're having a baby."

Excitement erupted. Everyone spoke at once. Allison was hugged again and again until she felt dizzy from being passed around.

"When's the baby due?" her mother-in-law asked as the hubbub died down.

"April," Allison answered.

"You'll need to find a bigger place to live. Your apartment is going to feel terribly small once there's a baby in the house."

Her father-in-law said, "Give them time, Lois."

"April will be here before any of us know it," Mom Kavanagh retorted. "I'm just trying to give them some good advice."

"You two, lay off," Tony said with a grin. "We'll figure this out. Won't we, Allie?"

She smiled at him, joy spilling over in her heart. "Yes."

A few hours later Allison wasn't feeling quite so happy when she looked at her husband. He was tipsy. Obviously so. She'd only seen him have one drink, when her father-in-law toasted the new baby. How many more had he had when she wasn't looking?

Once, in her first year of college, Allison had gone to a party with friends and had a few drinks. She hadn't liked the taste but she'd hated the way it made her feel later even more. The next morning she'd sworn off alcohol for good. It hadn't bothered her when Tony had the occasional drink, but then, she'd never seen him like this.

Before they left her in-laws' home, Mom Kavanagh pulled Allison aside. "You'd better drive home. Tony doesn't seem to be feeling well."

Not feeling well?

"You'd better send him to bed the minute you get home. I hope it wasn't something he ate. Food poisoning would be terrible for all of us."

Allison nodded. Was it food rather than alcohol that made Tony look and sound like that?

"If you get sick," her mother-in-law continued, "you call the doctor right away. You don't want to risk anything happening to the baby. Promise you will?"

"I'm feeling fine, but I promise to call the doctor if I need to."

Mom Kavanagh kissed Allison's cheek. "I am thrilled for you both, dear. Now you get on home and put your husband to bed."

Some of the tension left Allison. If Tony's mother wasn't worried, then she wouldn't be either.

Allison

Perhaps it was knowing her mother was praying for her that made Allison get up on Sunday morning and drive into Kings Meadow to attend church. Or perhaps it was knowing church was still the best place to meet the kind of people she wanted to know. Especially since she wouldn't cross the threshold of a bar for any reason. There weren't a whole lot of other options in a town this size.

In Boise she and Tony had been members of the same non-denominational fellowship since before Meredith was born. But Allison had attended less and less often after Tony walked out on her. It wasn't because she'd stopped believing in God. It wasn't because she'd turned her back on Christ. It wasn't even because she felt judged by anyone in the church, before or after they'd divorced. In fact, people had been nothing but kind and supportive. Still, she'd felt like a failure.

She'd failed at marriage.

She'd failed as a wife.

She'd failed as a believer.

She'd failed. Period.

The dirt and gravel parking lot at the side of the simple brick church building was filled with an odd assortment of vehicles, ranging from an enormous 1950s Cadillac, seemingly held together with duct tape, to a bright red, late-model Ferrari convertible. Mostly there were beat-up pickup trucks, primer but no paint, and monster four-wheel-drive diesels that must have cost as much as she earned in a year.

Allison had arrived on the late side, perhaps five minutes after the start of the worship service. She slipped into the last row of padded chairs while the congregation sang a contemporary worship song. The woman at the opposite end of the row smiled and nodded in her direction. Allison returned it before training her eyes on the overhead screen. Not that she needed to read the words. She knew the song by heart. It was one that had comforted her countless times as she walked through the desert place.

The worship team on the stage—the lead singer, a young woman with a guitar, another woman on the keyboard, and a teenage boy on the drums—moved smoothly into another song and then one more before ending in a word of prayer.

Allison anticipated the time of greeting that would follow the prayer, and she was prepared for everyone who shook hands with her to welcome her and say how nice it was to meet Emma Carter's niece. Everyone would know who she was. It was hard to stay anonymous in a small church just as it was hard to stay anonymous in a small town. What surprised her was that she *felt* welcome.

After the greeting time the offering was taken and announcements given, and then the pastor came to the pulpit. He was a tall beanpole of a man, perhaps in his late thirties or early forties. He had a pleasant speaking voice, and his teaching style drew Allison into the text. By the time the sermon was over, she was convinced she would return. Not that she was ready to commit herself to attending every Sunday. It was too soon for that. Still, her spirit felt lighter as she left the sanctuary.

Gizmo—who went almost everywhere with Allison, as long as the weather allowed—was glad to see her when she got to the car. She snapped on his leash, and the two of them walked down to the creek that ran behind the church building.

"Cute dog," a deep voice said.

Allison sucked in a gasp of surprise as she turned toward the speaker.

Standing back from the bank was an Idaho cowboy in all his glory, complete with boots, jeans, and black Stetson. He grinned as he dipped his chin in hello. "First time at Meadow Fellowship?"

"Yes." She hadn't noticed him inside the church. Had he been there? Must have since he seemed to know she'd been there.

"I'm guessing you're Allison Kavanagh, Miss Carter's niece."

See, everyone knew at least that much.

She answered, "Yes, but you have me at a disadvantage."

He removed his hat, revealing thick black hair with just a touch of gray at the temples. "Chet Leonard, ma'am. Pleased to make your acquaintance."

Allison felt her eyes widen. Did people still talk that way? Apparently up in these mountains they did.

"Actually, I had some help. Susan and Ned Lyle are friends of mine. Susan said she met you the other day when you came to town."

"Yes, we met. Does she go to this church? I didn't see her inside."

Chet Leonard shook his head. "No, the Lyles are Methodists. But I still hold 'em as friends."

She smiled, liking his sense of humor, but the smile felt awkward. How seldom she smiled these days. How seldom she laughed anymore. Really laughed. Tony used to make her—

"What's your dog's name?" Chet asked.

"Gizmo."

"Because of the ears?"

"Because of the ears."

He chuckled. She could barely hear it above the sound of flowing water.

"Dad?"

Chet looked up the incline toward the parking lot as a teen-ager—a younger version of Chet Leonard—stepped into view.

"You comin'?" the boy asked.

"I'm coming." Chet turned toward Allison again. "That's my son, Rick. I imagine he's starved and eager to go eat."

A wave of familiar loneliness washed over her. She ached for those times in the past when she'd been a part of a family. She'd loved going out to eat after church with Tony and Meredith. She'd loved being one-half of a couple, finishing Tony's sentences because she knew what he thought before he could say it.

Chet bent his hat brim in her direction. "It was a pleasure to meet you, Ms. Kavanagh."

"And you, Mr. Leonard," she answered softly, then turned to stare at the creek again, the good feelings she'd felt at the end of the church service forgotten.

Emma

1925

Alexander Monroe leaned across the table in the diner and took hold of Emma's hand. As usual, his touch caused her heart to beat faster. If only he wasn't oblivious to her feelings.

"Come on. Be a sport, Emma. Put in a good word for me with your sister."

Liza. Always his thoughts were on Liza. For three years it had been that way, Emma wanting Alexander and Alexander wanting Liza.

"It won't do any good. Liza's sweet on Matthew Steward." *This month, anyway.*

Alexander sighed as he released her hand and slouched against the back of the booth. "She drives me crazy, and she knows it too."

Yes, Liza knew she drove Alexander crazy. She drove *lots* of boys crazy. Alexander wasn't unique in that regard. Emma's sister loved to toy with boys the same way their tomcat loved to toy with mice. It was all a game to her, although she wasn't trying to hurt anyone. Liza hadn't a mean bone in her body.

But Emma wouldn't toy with Alexander. Not even by accident. She would treat him with tenderness. She would do anything to make him happy—even help him win Liza over. Emma loved Alexander Monroe. She'd started loving him on the night of the Hudsucker party and she'd learned to love him more with the passing of time, despite his indifference. He barely knew she was alive, let alone that she was a girl. Only enough to call her a sport and ask her to put in a good word for him with Liza.

Their mother liked to remind Emma and Liza that she was praying for their future husbands. "God has just the right man in store for you. Be patient and watch for him. He'll turn up, and you'll know it when you see him. That's how it was for me with your father."

Her mother was right. When Emma had first seen Alexander, she'd known he was the one for her. Apparently God hadn't told Alexander yet that she was the one for him. How could He tell him when Alexander never went to church? He had no time for God, he said.

Three months earlier Emma had graduated from high school. Fifteen of her female classmates had gotten married since then. Fifteen. There'd been fewer than fifty girls in the graduating class, and fifteen were married already. Two were expecting babies next year. And in those same three months, Liza had received two proposals of marriage even though she was only seventeen and had another year of schooling ahead of her.

Alexander intruded on Emma's thoughts. "Will you at least try? You know me. You like me. Tell her I'm a nice guy."

"I *have* told her." She looked out the window rather than let him see tears well in her eyes. It was bad enough he didn't care for her. It would be worse if he pitied her.

"Tell her again," he said.

"I will, but I can't promise it'll do any good."

Allison

Allison reached into the steamer trunk and, for the second time since discovering it, removed the bridal gown from the tissue paper it had been wrapped in. Then she dropped it over the dress form, carefully, as if clothing a bride on her wedding day.

The champagne-colored silk satin skirt was shin-length. Just right for the twenties. Matching champagne-colored beads and pearls embroidered the bodice and short puffy sleeves. Lovely and stylish, collectors of all things vintage would love to have it. But Allison had no intention of selling it. Something about it spoke to her heart.

Irrational, she supposed. She no longer had her own wedding dress. About ten years ago she'd given it away in a fit of anger. She'd wanted to hurt Tony. She should have known he wouldn't see the significance in her gesture. By that time he hadn't noticed much about her no matter what she did.

Allison and Tony had been married five years before she discovered how heavily he drank—a long time to keep that sort of secret. A few months later, at her insistence, he'd entered a thirty-day, in-patient recovery program, and she'd thought she would never have to worry about "that problem" raising its ugly head again.

How naive she'd been.

Two decades and the roller-coaster ride that was part and

parcel of a marriage to an active alcoholic had thoroughly disabused her of naiveté in that regard.

After Tony's first stint in rehab, Allison went on loving him, even when others thought her crazy to put up with him. Even when he lost another job and then another and another. Even when he landed in the hospital. Again and again. Even when he broke her heart and disappointed her and abandoned her emotionally. With his every new attempt at recovery, she took hold of hope and expected to see him overcome the desire to drink. She believed again and again that he would get sober and stay sober. Only to see him fail. Again.

One good thing came out of her troubled marriage: Allison had been driven to the foot of the cross. Her faith in Christ had been born and then challenged and deepened. A Bible study leader once said to her, "A faith that can't be tested can't be trusted." Well, Allison's faith had been thoroughly tested. She'd gone through the refiner's fire more than once.

And then, at long last, had come God's promise to save her marriage. Or at least she'd believed it was His voice, His promise at the time.

Tears sprang to her eyes at the memory. Disillusionment pierced her heart like the sting of a scorpion.

She'd been so certain God would heal her marriage, but it was clear that she'd misunderstood. For Allison's marriage was over and God did not lie.

She turned away from the bridal gown and the memories it had stirred to life and left the attic.

Taking a break from designing a logo for a client, Allison checked her e-mail, then opened her browser to the local Chamber of Commerce's website and began reading:

Kings Meadow, elevation 4,625 feet, is located in a long, wide valley surrounded by rugged mountains of southwestern Idaho. In the 1800s, the farmers and merchants who settled in this valley north of Boise City sold their produce, hogs, cows, and milk to the miners panning for gold throughout the Boise Basin. Eventually, the gold rush ended and most of the miners left the territory. But a good number of the farmers and merchants remained, and many of their descendants still live here today.

As she read, Allison pictured Chet Leonard, standing on the bank of the stream the previous Sunday. She wondered if his ancestors had settled in the valley over a hundred years before. He looked and sounded like a lifelong resident.

She shook her head, ridding herself of the image. She had no interest in men. Cowboys or not. Period. And that one had a family.

A glance at the clock told her it was time to take the dog for a walk. She slipped a sweatshirt over her head, put on her athletic shoes, and headed toward the door, leash in hand. Gizmo was waiting for her there.

In the two weeks since moving into the log house, Allison and Gizmo had explored several paths on their daily walks. Allison's favorite was the one that followed the river. And today, with wildflowers blooming everywhere—an abundance of pinks and blues, yellows and oranges—she felt a lifting of her spirit. It was so pretty. God's handprints were everywhere.

Thank You.

Her spirit lightened a little more.

Thank You that I had this place to come to. Thank You that I wasn't completely ruined in the divorce. I might've been. Other women have been. But I'm okay.

The simple prayer of thanksgiving broke through a barrier

in her heart, and something she couldn't quite define began to heal.

You've been with me every step of the way. Through the separation. Through the divorce. You were there all the time.

She didn't doubt for a moment that God had been with her. Still, she'd been shattered all the same, and the end of her dreams, the end of her marriage, had caused her to grow silent, to distrust her ability to hear God's voice.

Help me hear You again, Lord.

She stopped walking, giving Gizmo time to sniff the underbrush and explore each rock and cranny while giving her time to enjoy the scenery.

On this stretch of the river the water flowed by swiftly, its surface smooth, but behind her and around the bend was some of the best whitewater in the world. Rafters and kayakers flocked to this river every summer from around the globe. When Meredith was young, the family had gone on a rafting trip at least once every summer. More often if they had guests from out of state. Tony had loved to put "flatlanders," as he called those who were not from a mountainous area, in the front of the raft so they would get sprayed with the icy-cold water, drenching them before the trip downriver was over.

Tony's mischievous sense of humor was one of the things Allison had loved about him. He could make her laugh as no one else could. He'd also made her cry like no one else.

Not liking the direction of her thoughts—the second time today—she resumed walking.

Grieving was a process one had to go through—Allison knew this. It took as long as it took. But she didn't want grief to morph into self-pity. She'd never been that sort of person, not even at the worst of times. She didn't want to become that sort of person now. There was too much to be thankful for. She had a snug home in a gorgeous region. She had plenty of clients and a successful business. She had good health, and her parents and daughter were all well too.

But God hates divorce. The words pierced her heart—as they always did.

A month or so ago, when Allison had been in the deepest period of mourning, her mother reminded her that while the Bible said God hated divorce, He did not hate the *divorced*. God loved her and wanted His best for her. Her life was not over. God still had a purpose and a plan for her. All she had to do was trust Him.

She knew all of that in her mind. It was getting it into her heart that was so hard. She supposed, like grief, belief took time too.

Allison

On Friday evening a storm blew through the area, causing trees to dance like whirling dervishes and the wind to whistle beneath the eaves. It was a perfect night to sit before the living room fireplace, listening to the wood crackle and pop, while she sorted through more things from Aunt Emma's trunk.

It was the photographs that interested Allison the most, and there were lots of them. Far more than she'd first thought. Some of them had writing on the backs, identifying the people in the photograph, but others didn't. Of course, many of them were of Aunt Emma and Allison's grandmother, Elizabeth Hendricks, and their parents; she recognized all those family members easily enough. There were a lot of her mother as a baby, including some naked ones on a bear rug. Those shots made Allison laugh out loud. Wait until she told her mother about them.

After about an hour of looking, she decided organization was needed before anything else. She had some empty shoeboxes in the spare room upstairs. She would get them and start sorting photos into different boxes. One for photos of people she could identify. One for photos of people she couldn't identify. And one for photos that piqued her curiosity, made her want to know more.

"I wish I'd seen these before Aunt Emma died," she said aloud.

Gizmo lifted his head and stared at her.

"If I'd seen them then, I could have asked her. Especially about this guy." She held up another photo of her aunt with that same young man, the one she'd asked her mother about. Whoever he was, he was devastatingly handsome. Although the photograph was black and white, she was certain his eyes must have been a piercing blue, and there was a broodiness in his expression that made her think of Douglas Fairbanks, a silent film star from the twenties.

"Who was he to you, Aunt Emma?"

A gust of wind rattled the windows, startling Allison. She dropped the photo, and it drifted dangerously close to the fireplace before landing on the floor. She got up and retrieved it, then headed upstairs for the shoeboxes.

Emma

1926

Liza's June wedding to John Hendricks, eldest son of one of Idaho's leading—and wealthiest—citizens, was the social event of the summer. The pews of the church were filled with friends and family, successful businessmen and powerful government officials, both city and state. Everybody who was anybody had been invited to the wedding, and from the looks of the packed sanctuary, most had accepted the invitation.

Emma was delighted to serve as her sister's maid of honor, although she felt awkward and gauche whenever she stood next to Liza, who was even more stunning than usual in her long white satin gown and exquisite veil. Emma was thankful when, at last, she was able to slip away from the spotlight and observe the reception from a dim corner of the banquet hall the Hendricks had rented for the occasion. She wasn't surprised when Alexander joined her there.

"Well, she did it," he said, his gaze locked on the bride. "Landed herself a rich husband."

"She loves John."

"Does she?" Alexander turned his eyes on Emma. "I've started to believe Liza only loves herself."

"Don't say such things, Alexander. Not to me. She's my sister, and I only want her happiness. John makes her happy."

He cocked one eyebrow. "What has she ever done to deserve your unswerving loyalty?"

"Stop it."

"Really, Emma. I mean it. What has she ever done? Does she ever think of you first? Does she ever think of anybody but her—"

She frowned at him, then turned to walk away.

He grabbed her upper arm to stop her, pulling her around to face him again.

"I won't stay if you keep talking like that," she told him. "I won't listen to another negative word about Liza. This is her wedding day."

"All right. I'll be quiet."

"Promise?"

"Promise."

She was glad he promised because she didn't want to leave this corner. And she didn't want to leave Alexander's side either.

The small orchestra on the stage played a few notes to get the attention of the guests. When the room fell silent, Liza and her groom moved to the center of the floor. The bride held her train over her right forearm, and as John drew her into his embrace, Liza smiled up at him with adoration. What a handsome couple they made. They belonged together, John and Liza.

A lump formed in Emma's throat.

"Come on, Emma," Alexander said. "We might as well join them. You can waltz, can't you?"

"Yes, I can waltz."

It was the first time Alexander held her in his arms, and as they moved around the room with the other couples, she pretended not to know he'd rather be holding her sister.

Allison

Susan Lyle was a force of nature. She was sixty-two but she had the energy of a woman half her age. It took no time at all for Allison to consider Susan the best friend she'd ever had.

The two women fell into a habit of meeting for coffee on Friday mornings at a little Kings Meadow bistro on Main Street. Allison felt so comfortable with Susan that she'd soon shared more details about her marriage with her new friend than she'd shared with her counselor or her codependency group after more than a year with them. In addition to learning each other's life stories, they spent a fair amount of time talking about God. Allison looked forward to those conversations the most. Susan's faith was deep and unwavering, and Allison drank in her words of wisdom as she felt her own faith strengthen and grow.

When Susan invited her to join the book club that met at the library on the third Monday of every month, Allison agreed without hesitation. She hadn't read books for fun in recent years. The book club, she hoped, would reintroduce her to reading a story for pure pleasure. It would also help her break the habit of vegging in front of cable television after a day at the computer. And besides, it was an opportunity to meet more of her neighbors—neighbors being a loose term in these mountains.

By the end of her first summer as a full-time resident, Allison had stopped thinking of the log house as Aunt Emma's place. It had become her home. Sure, there were times when she missed the life she'd had in Boise with Tony and Meredith. Times when she missed the ease of finding whatever she wanted at the grocery store or at the mall. And there were nights when she reached her hand across to the empty side of the bed, wishing it wasn't her dog she found there. But for the most part, she was content. Happy, even. She felt healthier—physically, emotionally, and spiritually.

Perhaps she even felt fresh hope for the future.

Returning from her walk with Gizmo one afternoon in mid-September, Allison told herself she must start taking her camera everywhere she went. The colors had started to turn, and autumn would become more beautiful with every passing day. She didn't want to miss any of it. Maybe she should buy a book on nature photography—one of those manuals written for dummies—and see if she could become proficient, at least to a small degree. Aunt Emma had made her living with photography. Perhaps Allison had inherited a little of that talent.

As she climbed the steps to the deck, she heard the phone ringing inside. She hurried to unlock the door and grab it before it went to voice mail. "Hello?"

"Mom?"

"Hi, honey. What a nice surprise to hear your voice."

"Mom, I got a call from St. Luke's. Dad's in the ER. They think it's his pancreas again. It sounds like he's in bad shape."

Bad shape. Did she mean drunk?

"Can you drive down there? I'm worried and I don't know when anyone at the hospital will let me know how he's doing."

Chaos. Allison had grown used to its absence. "Oh, Meredith. I—"

"I know, Mom. I don't blame you for not wanting to go. But I'm so far away, and he *is* my dad."

She had no argument against such words. "All right. I'll leave as soon as I change my clothes and put on some makeup."

"Call me when you know anything. I'll have my cell phone with me all the time."

"I will. I'll call as soon as I have something to share."

"Thanks, Mom."

Allison hung up the phone. She was glad her daughter had been mending fences with her father over the summer. Once Meredith was old enough to understand, Allison had been honest with her about her dad's problem. Allison had encouraged Meredith to love Tony unconditionally but never to enable him. She'd tried to set that example, although she'd often failed at it.

The phone rang again before she could step away from it. This time she checked the caller ID before picking up the handset. "Hi, Susan," she answered as she walked toward her bedroom.

"Allison, I'm calling about book club. Could you—"

"Sorry," she interrupted her friend. "I don't think I'll be there tonight. I've got to go down to Boise. I'm getting ready to leave as we speak."

"Is something wrong?"

"It's Tony. He's in the hospital."

"Oh, Allison. Would you like company? I'd be glad to join you if you need me. I'm not leading the discussion at book club, so I don't have to be there."

Allison felt torn. On one hand, she would love to have Susan's company. On the other, she wasn't sure she wanted her friend to see Tony. Though why it should matter, she didn't know. He was her ex. She wasn't responsible for him or for what he did or for how he looked or for what others thought about him.

"Let me pray for you," Susan said.

Allison's throat tightened. She wasn't about to turn down

prayer, but the kindness of the gesture made her want to cry. "Okay." She closed her eyes.

Her friend's words were few, but they seemed to lift a weight Allison hadn't realized was pressing upon her.

"I could be at your place in less than fifteen minutes if you want me to go with you," Susan added.

"No. It's sweet of you, but I think I'd rather go alone. I don't know how long I'll be down there. It could be really late before I get home."

"What about Gizmo?"

"I'll take him with me. I can leave him in the car."

"It's hotter down in the valley than here."

True. She hadn't thought of that. She couldn't safely leave him in the car for any length of time. September in Boise could be as hot as July.

"Listen," Susan said, "you gave me the key to your house and the code for your alarm. You go on, and I'll take care of the dog. He can stay with me for the night."

"Oh, Susan. That's asking way too—"

"You didn't ask. I offered."

More kindness. Allison drew in a shaky breath and let it out slowly. "Okay. If you're sure."

"I'm sure. And I'll keep praying for you."

"Thanks."

———

Allison had grown to hate hospitals. She hated the sounds. She hated the smells. She hated the anxiety that rose up inside her as she entered the lobby through the automatic glass doors.

At the information desk she learned Tony had been admitted and was given his room number. She didn't bother to ask about his condition. Even if the volunteer behind the desk knew the answer, she wouldn't have told her. Privacy laws didn't allow it.

On the ride up in the elevator, she tried to remember the words of Susan's prayer. She reminded herself she was there for Meredith's sake. Not for her own sake and not for Tony's. She was there for Meredith. Period.

But the self-talk didn't help much.

She found Tony's room at the end of a long hallway. The door was half open, and she had to step around a drawn curtain before she could see the bed and Tony in it.

Memories from the past crashed over her. So many trips to the hospital during the years of their marriage. So many that they ran together in her head until she couldn't distinguish one from another. She didn't want to be in this hospital room. She didn't want to ever look at Tony in a hospital bed again. She needed to leave. She couldn't—

He opened his eyes and saw her. "Allie," he said softly, offering a wobbly smile.

"Meredith called me." She needed him to know that was the only reason she'd come.

"She's a good kid."

Reluctantly, Allison moved to the side of the bed. "Yes, she is."

He grimaced, as if in pain, but she could tell he was heavily sedated.

"She said it might be your pancreas again."

"Yeah. Looks like it."

Allison didn't have to ask if it was because he'd been drinking. She knew the signs. She'd seen him like this before. She wanted to remind him he could die from pancreatitis and ask him why he was so stupid. Didn't he realize he was killing himself by inches?

It isn't my business. It isn't my business. It isn't my business.

Tony said, "Tell Meredith I'll probably be out by the weekend, if all goes well."

"Okay."

"Tell her I'll call her in a couple of days when I'm feeling a little better."

Will you feel better, Tony? For how long? Why don't you stop drinking? Why? Our lives could have been so different if not for your drinking. Why did you have to throw it all away?

His eyes drifted closed again. "I'm glad you came, Allie," he mumbled as he drifted back to sleep.

She waited awhile, then went outside to call Meredith, as promised. Her daughter answered on the first ring.

"How is he, Mom?"

"He's in pain but he says he should be out by the weekend." She drew in a deep breath, tamping down an old anger. "He's been through this before. It usually takes about a week in the hospital, and then he'll have to be very careful with his diet."

"Do you think he will be? Careful, I mean."

"Oh, honey. I don't know. You know how it is for your dad."

"Yeah. I know."

It was at moments like these when Allison wanted to hate Tony Kavanagh, but she couldn't. She didn't like him much, but she couldn't hate him. "He's always pulled through before," she said at last. It was the best she could do and still be telling the truth.

Allison

It was after midnight before Allison crawled beneath the covers of her bed. Exhausted by the events of the day, she fell into a troubled sleep. In her dreams, she stood beside an open grave. Tony's grave. Meredith gripped her arm. Both of them wept.

What could I have done?

What could I have done?

What could I have done?

Allison bolted upright with a gasp, heart racing, fear strangling her. But as her pulse began to slow, anger surged. She shouldn't have to visit Tony in the hospital. She shouldn't have to dream about him. He'd made his choices. What he did shouldn't matter to her any longer. Not even if it killed him. And if it wasn't for their daughter—

A groan rumbled in her chest as she tossed aside the covers and got out of bed. The clock said it was four in the morning, but she wouldn't fall back to sleep again. She was too agitated for that. Might as well get some work done.

But remnants of the dream stayed with her as she showered and dressed and made her first cup of coffee. They stayed with her as she opened Photoshop and set to work on another logo design. They were still clinging to her thoughts when a knock sounded at the door a little after nine o'clock.

It was Susan, returning Gizmo.

"Was he a good dog?" Allison asked as she held him in her arms and ruffled his ears.

"Yes. Although I think all the attention he got put my dogs' noses out of joint. The big lugs aren't allowed on the furniture the way Gizmo is."

"Want some coffee?"

"Sure."

The two women walked to the kitchen.

Allison pulled open the tray beneath her coffeemaker. "Full strength, half caf, or decaf?"

"Full strength, please."

"Full it is." She grabbed a K-Cup.

After the coffee started flowing into a mug, Allison turned toward her friend. "I sure appreciated your help. It was good not to have to worry about Gizmo."

"How was seeing Tony?"

"Harder than I expected." She shrugged. "It brought up so many raw feelings. I thought I was finished with them, but I guess not."

"You and Tony were married a long time. You loved him. Maybe those feelings won't ever go away completely."

"I hope you're wrong. I want to move on."

Allison set the mug of coffee on the counter, then got the flavored creamer out of the refrigerator. While Susan doctored her coffee, Allison went to retrieve her own mug from her desk in the bedroom. By the time Allison returned to the kitchen and got her own coffee, Susan had taken a seat at the table. They were silent for a short while as they sipped.

"I dreamed again that he died," Allison said at long last, her gaze fastened on the mug in her hands.

"Is he that ill?"

Allison shrugged, then shook her head. "Not that anyone told me. But pancreatitis is a serious condition. It could kill him." Tears stung her eyes and her throat tightened. She fought both reactions.

"It's okay to care about him, Allison."

"I'm not sure I do care. I was crying in my dream, but I don't think I was crying for him. Not really." She drew in a deep breath. "Do you think God told me to let go of Tony because he *is* going to die?"

"Oh, Allison."

"What if I didn't hear God right about that either?" she whispered.

Susan shook her head. "No one can answer that question except you. And maybe you won't be able to answer it for a long time. But I can tell you this: Feelings aren't right or wrong. They're just feelings. They just *are*. What matters is what you do in response to those feelings. Let God do His work in your heart, Allison. He will turn things to good in your life when you follow Him. Even divorce."

Was that true? Allison swallowed the lump a second time. *Please, Father. Do Your work in my heart. Forgive me for my own wrong choices. Turn this mess . . . turn all of these crazy, confusing emotions into good in my life . . . And please don't let Tony die. Not yet. Not until he surrenders completely to You.*

Allison

Ned Lyle's sixty-fifth birthday party was held the following Saturday. Allison arrived at the Lyle home half an hour before the other guests, sheet cake in hand. While Susan put the last-minute touches on the meal she'd made, Allison stuck candles into the cake. One for every year of the birthday boy's life, plus a couple dozen more for good measure. Several of them were the kind of candles that couldn't be blown out.

"Mean, aren't we?" Susan said softly from the opposite side of the counter.

"Deliciously wicked," Allison confirmed with a laugh.

"What are you two up to?" Ned stepped through the doorway to the dining room.

Allison turned around and stationed her body between him and the cake. "You were told not to come into the kitchen."

"Like I was going to obey that command."

Chet Leonard appeared in the doorway behind Ned. "Need help?"

Ned nodded. "Probably."

"I meant the ladies."

"Traitor," Ned said with a grin. Then he raised his hands in a gesture of surrender. "All right. I'm going. I'm going."

After Ned left the kitchen, Chet said, "I meant it. Need any help from me?"

"Nothing I can think of," Susan answered. "Allison?"

"Nope. The candles are all in place. But maybe we should put the volunteer fire department on alert. We're going to have quite the blaze when these are all lit." Allison closed the lid on the empty box that the sheet cake had come in from the grocery store, then looked at Chet again. "Try to keep Ned from peeking until it's time for dessert."

Chet winked. "You got it."

Chet hadn't been gone more than a minute when his wife, Marsha, came through the same doorway.

"Chet says you don't need help, but I thought I should check."

Washing her hands in the sink, Susan looked over her shoulder. "It's all ready. As soon as everyone's here, we can eat."

"There's quite the crowd outside," Marsha responded.

Susan dried her hands on a towel. "I'll do a quick headcount." She left the kitchen.

Marsha pretended to count the candles on the cake. "Oh my."

Allison laughed.

"Susan's always been the mischievous one."

"That's what I've discovered." Allison sat on a nearby barstool.

Marsha leaned her hip against the counter. "You seem to have settled in well."

"I think so. I like living here more than I thought I would."

"I hope you don't get cabin fever in the winter. I do. There's times every winter when I'd give just about anything to move to a warmer climate where there aren't icy roads and too much snow to shovel. But it would take a cannon to blast Chet out of Kings Meadow."

Did Allison hear a tinge of irritation in the other woman's words? She couldn't be sure.

Marsha waved a hand, as if chasing away a pesky fly. "Don't mind me. I just know that it's warm today but we could get our first snowfall any day."

"Really? This early?"

"Trust me. It can be this early. You never know in these mountains."

Would Allison suffer from cabin fever? Aunt Emma hadn't. She used to say winter was when she got the most work done, and that allowed her to play more in the summer. Allison remembered the smell of chemicals seeping under the door from the darkroom where her aunt developed her photographs, and it made her smile.

I'll just hope I'm more like Aunt Emma and less like Marsha Leonard.

Susan reentered the kitchen, putting an end to the brief conversation. "Everyone's here. Chet's going to bless the food. Come on outside."

The rest of the afternoon passed pleasantly. Allison made a few new acquaintances and enjoyed the company of others she'd met already over the summer. Over dessert, she took particular interest when several men, including Ned and Chet, got into a debate regarding the timing of a bank robbery in Kings Meadow in the previous century.

"I'm telling you," Ned said, "that didn't happen in the thirties. It happened during the second World War."

Chet shook his head. "You're wrong. It was during the Great Depression."

"Where's your boy?" a man whose name Allison had momentarily forgotten asked. "Rick'll know. They cover that in high school history."

Chet straightened and looked around. "I don't see him. Must be inside or maybe down at the barn." Then his gaze fell on Allison. "If your aunt were here, she could tell us. Emma Carter knew the history of this area as well as any historian."

The other men nodded.

Allison smiled. "Yes, she did. I always loved her stories about Kings Meadow."

"Folks up here have always appreciated a good storyteller," Chet said, returning her smile. "And your aunt was the best story-teller I ever heard."

His comment warmed Allison's heart. She'd thought the same about Aunt Emma, and it delighted her to hear someone else say so.

Emma

1926

Emma was working on needlepoint—at her mother's insistence—when Liza burst into the parlor. Always beautiful with her blond hair, blue eyes, pale complexion, and a lithe figure that seemed custom ordered for the current fashions, Liza absolutely glowed with happiness as she joined her sister on the settee.

Emma set aside her needlework, glad for an excuse to stop. Even more glad to spend time alone with her younger sister. There were too few opportunities these days. Liza rarely went anywhere without her husband. Emma missed those many nights when the two sisters would lie awake, talking, sharing secrets, giggling about something that happened at school. With Liza married and setting up a home of her own, Emma felt as though a part of her was missing. To make matters worse, now their mother's attention was totally focused on her elder daughter's unmarried state. As if Emma needed Mama's constant reminders of the many ways she failed.

Liza took hold of Emma's hand and squeezed her fingers. "You will never guess my news."

"What is it?"

"Guess."

Irritation—but with her mother, not with Liza—made her jaw twitch. "Why should I try if you say I will never guess it?"

Liza wasn't fazed by Emma's ill humor. In fact, her smile

broadened. "Okay. I'll tell you. I've seen the doctor and I'm going to have a baby."

"A baby? Already?"

"You sound surprised. John and I have been married almost three months." Liza laughed. Then her voice dropped to a whisper, even though they were alone in the room. "The truth is, I must have gotten pregnant on our honeymoon. We couldn't get enough of each other. Still can't."

Embarrassment caused Emma's face to grow hot. She was a virgin, but she understood the essentials when it came to conception.

"Be happy for me, Emma."

"Of course I'm happy. I'm going to be an aunt." *But I don't want to be an old maid aunt.*

"You mustn't tell anyone. I haven't told John yet, but I couldn't wait to tell you."

Emma had never allowed herself to envy her younger sister before, but she had to fight both envy and resentment now. Couldn't something good happen to *her* sometimes? Couldn't a man learn to love and adore *her*? Couldn't Alexander learn to love her? Would *she* ever have the joy of announcing that she was expecting a baby?

"Don't even tell Mother," Liza added. "Promise me."

"I promise. I won't say a word to anyone."

"Good." Her sister rose to her feet. "Now I must go home. I've planned a very special meal for tonight, and I want to make sure all is in readiness."

Before Liza could move away, Emma stood and drew her into a tight hug. "Thank you for telling me. I'm happy for you and John. Very happy."

"I knew you would be." Liza kissed Emma's cheek. "Tell Mother I couldn't stay but I will come for a nice long visit tomorrow. In fact, tell her John and I are coming for supper. She might guess what that means, but tell her anyway." Liza said her farewell over her shoulder as she hurried out of the parlor.

Emma *was* happy for her sister. Truly, she was. Liza couldn't help that good things came her way all the time any more than she could help being beautiful.

But still . . .

Allison

The first snow flurries of the season were falling on that Saturday in October when Allison discovered the leather-bound journals in the bottom of the second trunk in the attic. She'd thought the photographs—some of which she'd framed, others she'd placed in scrapbooks, many she was still trying to organize—would be what she treasured most. But these journals were like pure gold to her. How wonderful that her gifted, storytelling aunt had written down events from her life.

After looking through them Allison realized her great-aunt had kept journals faithfully from the time she was a girl of fifteen until the year she entered the care center at the age of ninety-seven. There were over forty of them, unlined pages filled with Aunt Emma's particular hand. The dates covered inside had been written on the blank fly page in the front of each journal, making it easy to stack them in order. That was how Allison planned to read them. Like a series of wonderful novels.

As she withdrew the last of the journals from the trunk, she thought of the mystery man in her aunt's photographs. It was tempting to look ahead in the journals to discover his identity, but she resisted the urge. She wanted to savor the story of Emma Carter's life. But she did wonder why her aunt hadn't told her about the journals. She must have known Allison would find them eventually.

Glancing up from the leather book in her hand, she saw that the snow was falling harder now. She got up from the floor and walked to the window. A white carpet covered the ground. Already a couple of inches deep, with no signs of it stopping soon.

Time to fire up the treadmill. Her long walks with Gizmo would be less frequent in the coming months. Allison wasn't a fan of the cold or the snow, and her small dog wasn't crazy about the white stuff either. She could only hope the two of them wouldn't get cabin fever, like Marsha Leonard had warned, before spring arrived in earnest.

At least I have plenty to read while I wait for the spring thaw.

Allison returned to the stacks of journals next to the trunks and picked up an armful of them, starting with the oldest ones. Then she carried the books down to her bedroom on the first floor. There, she placed them on a bookcase on the right side of her bed.

What she wanted to do was grab the first one, go lie on the sofa with a blanket over her lap, and read to her heart's content. But this was Saturday, and she needed to do some housework before she got lazy. Starting with mopping the kitchen floor. It amazed her how one woman and a small dog could mess up a house so quickly.

Disorder used to bother Allison a lot. She supposed it was another control issue. Certainly she'd blamed Tony for any disorder that came into their lives. What was it the Bible said? A contentious woman was like a steady drip of water on a rainy day. Something like that. If Allison was brutally honest with herself, she would admit she'd been that contentious woman plenty of times throughout her marriage.

Okay, she *would* admit it. She hadn't been the perfect, loving, giving, charitable, praying wife she should have been. But who could have been such a paragon of virtue, married to Tony Kavanagh?

Is that a speck in your eye, Allison, or is it a log?

The thought made her angry. She grabbed the broom from the utility closet and attacked the kitchen floor with a vengeance.

Emma

Emma hadn't seen Alexander in over five months. Not since before Thanksgiving. There had been times when she'd thought she might die from missing him. Only she hadn't died. She'd gone on living . . . and hurting.

Thus, when she opened the front door one evening in April, she was more than a little surprised to see him standing there.

"Hi, Em. How you been?"

"Fine." A lie if ever there was one.

"Can we talk?" With a tip of his head he indicated she should come outside. "Out here. In private."

She nodded and stepped through the open doorway, closing the door behind her.

"How's the family?" he asked as he followed her toward the porch swing.

"Everyone's fine."

"I heard your sister had a baby."

Liza. Of course. He wanted to know about Liza. "Yes. A little boy. They named him John Jr." She sat on the swing and gave a little push with her foot, setting it in motion.

Alexander leaned his behind against the porch railing. "She still in love with her husband?"

"What kind of question is that? Of course she is."

He shrugged. "Sometimes people change their minds. Sometimes folks get divorced."

"Not people in the Carter family." Emma stopped the swing and sat straighter. "Mother would expire from the very thought of it. Liza would never divorce John even if she didn't love him. But she does love him, so it doesn't matter."

"Yeah. I guess not."

Emma looked away from him and stared out at the quiet street that ran in front of her home. Many of the trees were green with new leaves. Others were covered in buds, saying they weren't far behind. Tulips and crocuses were in bloom near the porch steps.

"Em?"

"Hmm."

"Why don't we get married?"

Her eyes widened. "What?"

"I asked you to marry me."

But you don't love me.

"Why shouldn't we get married? We've known each other for years. We get along good. You don't have a fella and I don't have any special girl. No point us going on alone, you stuck here with your parents. I've got a bit of money put away. Enough for a nice honeymoon. We could go off somewhere and have fun. Forget Boise for a while."

He meant *forget Liza.* Emma knew it as surely as she knew her own name. But if they were married, maybe he *would* forget Liza eventually. Maybe Emma could make him forget her sister once and for all. Maybe she could teach him to love her.

"When?" she asked softly.

"When what?"

"When would you want to get married?"

He grinned as he pushed off the railing. "As soon as possible. We could elope tomorrow if you want."

"No." She shook her head. "I don't want to elope. I'd like to have a wedding."

Alexander frowned. "No big production."

Of course. He was remembering Liza's wedding.

She answered, "No, nothing fancy. A quiet ceremony, here at home. Early June, perhaps."

Alexander came to the swing and sat beside her. "A few more weeks won't matter much. I can wait." Then he leaned over and brushed his lips against hers.

Their first kiss and it was over in an instant. But soon she would be his wife and she could kiss him as often and for as long as she wished.

"So you'll do it?" he asked, drawing back from her. "You'll marry me?"

"Yes, Alexander. I'll marry you."

Allison

The snow was gone by the time Allison left for church the next morning, but there was still a bite in the wind blowing through the canyon. Cold enough that Allison decided to leave Gizmo at home.

As she drove toward Kings Meadow, Allison wondered how many times during the coming winter months she might be forced to stay home because of slick roads. Hopefully not often. Attending the worship services at Meadow Fellowship had become one of the high points of her week. A healing had been taking place while she sat in the back row of the small sanctuary, Sunday after Sunday. A healing in her spirit. A healing not yet complete but getting there.

When Allison pulled into the parking lot, she saw a group of people standing outside the church entrance, almost in a huddle. Why didn't they go inside out of the wind? It seemed strange on such a cold morning. She got out of her Subaru and walked toward them.

One of the women turned as Allison approached. It was Sarah Parker, the women's ministry leader. Her face was streaked with tears.

Allison felt her heart sink. Something bad had happened. "Sarah? What's wrong?"

"Chet and Marsha Leonard's son was killed last night."

"Rick?"

Sarah nodded.

Allison pressed a hand against her chest. Rick, the eldest of the three Leonard children, had been such a bright and likable young man. A cowboy like his father, and so good-looking he must have driven the girls crazy.

"What happened?" she asked.

"A car accident. He and three other boys were driving back from Boise last night. The car hit black ice. It slid off the road and went into the river. Rick didn't get out."

Hearing such news made her think of her own child. How grateful she was Meredith had come through her teen years without having some horrid accident or ailment. But she quickly pushed the thought away. "What about the other boys?"

"Two are in the hospital in Boise. The third was able to come home last night with his parents."

Allison looked toward the entrance, then back again. "Are Chet and Marsha inside?"

"No." Sarah shook her head. "They stayed in Boise overnight with Marsha's parents."

She heard singing through the closed church door: "It is well . . . with my soul . . ."

The words of the hymn caused tears to well in Allison's eyes.

Sarah added, "The women's ministry will take them some prepared meals when the Leonards return home."

"Let me know how I can help."

"I will."

After that, the small group moved inside.

That morning's usual order of service was discarded. The congregation sang a little. They prayed a lot. Women wept. Men fought tears too. The pastor didn't give his prepared sermon. Instead, he ministered to his small flock with words of comfort from the Bible and words of wisdom gleaned from years in the ministry.

Allison was exhausted by the time church let out. But instead of driving home, she turned her car toward Susan's house. If Allison was heartbroken over Chet and Marsha's loss, she knew Susan's grief would be ten times worse. But it turned out Allison couldn't be of any comfort to Susan because she had gone with her husband to Boise to console the Leonard family.

Allison drove home, and after letting Gizmo outside, she settled onto the sofa in front of the fireplace. Then she called Meredith.

"Hi, Mom."

Allison felt ridiculously close to tears at the sound of her daughter's voice. "Hey, sweetheart. How are you?"

"I'm fine. Some friends and I are going to the zoo this afternoon. I'm waiting for them to come pick me up."

"The zoo. That sounds like fun."

"It's a great one. You need to come down for a visit so we can go together."

What Allison wouldn't give to be able to hug Meredith right that moment. To pull her close and feel her heart beat. Life felt more fragile than usual. She was all too aware how quickly anyone she cared about could be gone.

"Mom?"

"I'm sorry, honey."

"Are you crying?"

"No. Yes. A little."

"What happened? Is it Dad?"

"It isn't your father." Exasperation caused Allison to press her lips together while drawing a deep breath through her nostrils. Everything wasn't about Tony. Her daughter needed to learn that, just as she'd had to. She released the breath and said, "A boy who goes to my church was killed in a car accident last night. So young. Seventeen years old. It just . . . it just hit me kind of hard."

"Oh, Mom. I'm sorry."

"I needed to hear your voice."

"I'm okay, Mom. Honest. I'm careful when I go out. I look both ways when I cross the street. I eat my vegetables. I get enough sleep and plenty of exercise."

The loving note in Meredith's voice helped chase away Allison's negative feelings.

"Wish I could be there with you," her daughter added.

"Me too."

Allison heard the faint chime of a doorbell.

"Mom, I've gotta go. My friends are here. You going to be all right?"

"I'm fine, honey. Go enjoy the zoo."

"Okay. I'll call you later."

They said good-bye and Allison hung up the phone. She thought about a number of different things she could do to fill her afternoon. But in the end, she pulled a throw off the back of the sofa, lay down, and took a nap.

Emma

Alexander and Emma were married in her parents' front parlor on June 9, 1927. Only a few family members were in attendance. After the splash of Liza's wedding the previous year, the ceremony seemed a bit drab, but it was the way they wanted it. Simple. No fuss.

The newlyweds honeymooned in New York City, and along with four million other people, they watched Charles Lindbergh's ticker-tape parade up Broadway, celebrating the aviator's successful flight across the Atlantic.

Emma described all of the sights and sounds of the parade in her journal that night, but she was certain she would never forget any of it. Not the snow-flurry of paper falling from the windows of tall buildings. Not the sense of excitement in the crowds on the street below. Definitely not the moment when she caught a glimpse of Lindbergh himself, waving as the car he rode in passed by.

"Why do you do that?" Alexander asked her.

She looked up from the journal. "Do what?"

"Write in that book all the time."

"I want to remember. I love to look back in my diaries and recall what's happened in my life. The things I've learned. How I felt."

"Do you write about me?" He grinned.

She returned the smile. "Of course."

"Have you written about our honeymoon? You know." He motioned with his head toward the bed, his meaning clear.

Heat flooded her cheeks.

Alexander rose from his chair and approached the small desk. "I think I'd better read what you have to say about me."

"No, Alexander." She closed the journal, not caring that the ink was still wet and would smudge. "A diary is a private matter."

"I'm your husband. You shouldn't keep any secrets from me."

"I'm not keeping secrets." She pulled the book against her chest, clutching it with both hands. "It's just *private*."

His grin vanished in an instant. So fast, she wondered if she'd imagined it in the first place. "I want to read it."

Seeing his anger, a shiver raced up her spine.

"Give it here, Emma." He held out his hand. "Don't be stubborn."

She shouldn't be stubborn. What did it matter if he read it? All he would find were glowing words about how much she loved him. How much she'd always loved him. How happy she was now that they were married. How she delighted in his touch when he took her into his arms.

"Emma, hand it over." There was a cold, hard edge in his voice.

She gave him the journal, though doing so felt like a betrayal to herself.

Allison

Just about everybody who lived in or near Kings Meadow—or so it seemed—turned out for the funeral of Rick Leonard. The teenager had been popular among his peers, and his parents were loved and respected in the community. Allison hadn't known the boy all his life, as others had, but that didn't make the service any easier to go through. It was a wrenching thing, a memorial for a young man gone too soon.

The Leonards—Chet, Marsha, Rick's two younger brothers, and an older couple whom Allison assumed were the grand-parents—sat in the front pew in Meadow Fellowship Church. Chet had his right arm around his wife's shoulders, and every so often her body shuddered. Even from the last pew where Allison sat, she knew Marsha was keening on the inside. Susan had said her friend was inconsolable. Allison believed it.

The service wasn't much longer than half an hour. The reverend spoke for awhile. Rick's grandfather said a few words on behalf of the family. A teenage girl sang a song Allison didn't know but that moved her deeply. And always she was aware of the shudders of Marsha's grief, shaking her again and again.

Mourners left Meadow Fellowship and gathered to eat and console one another in the gymnasium of the high school where classes had been canceled for the day. Allison had volunteered to be one of the servers, and so she took her place as directed at one of the long tables. There, she scooped two different casseroles onto plates as people passed by. She was thankful for the job. It kept her from dwelling too much on the sorrow of the day.

She remained with Susan to clean up after most had returned to their homes.

"You've been a godsend," Susan told her as they tightened plastic ties around the tops of garbage bags filled with paper plates and cups.

"I'm glad I could be of use."

"Marsha and Chet are grateful for everyone who pitched in to help."

"I wish there was more I could do for them."

"I know. Me too. But for now, we'll have to trust that the Comforter will see them through the coming days."

Allison nodded. The Holy Spirit had been with her through many trials during her lifetime. Sometimes she'd been physically and emotionally aware of His aid and comfort. Sometimes she'd believed in His care by faith alone. She prayed it would be the former for the Leonards.

With the cleanup completed, the two women gave each other a warm hug and bid farewell. Then Allison returned home.

Gizmo was overjoyed to see her. She let him outside, but she decided to skip their usual walk. She was exhausted and the beckoning sofa was too much to resist. After dropping a favorite movie into the Blu-ray player, she pulled the soft throw off the back of the couch and lay down. It wasn't long before her eyes were drifting closed. The movie became a kind of white noise, lulling her to sleep.

When she awakened, the light coming through the living room windows had dimmed and the movie was over. Allison yawned as she sat up. Gizmo moved to sit in front of her, leveling a beseeching gaze at her.

"Need out, fella?"

He darted to the front door.

Allison smiled as she stood. "Okay. Okay. I'm coming." She grabbed the throw to wrap around her shoulders and went out onto the deck to wait for him. *Thanks, Lord, for little dogs who can bring a smile even when there are reasons to be sad.*

Gizmo barked at something stirring in the underbrush. Never sure if there might be something dangerous lurking where she couldn't see, Allison called to Gizmo. Thankfully, the obedience training she'd invested in when he was a puppy had been top-notch. He might want to chase whatever wild creatures were out there—mostly squirrels and chipmunks—but he always came when she called.

"Let's get something to eat," she said, and mistress and dog returned indoors.

As Allison headed for the kitchen, she realized how hungry she was. She'd stayed so busy serving at the high school she'd forgotten to eat anything herself. She opened the refrigerator and stared at the shelves. Something quick and easy was in order. She settled for cheese and crackers and a dill pickle. Not the most nutritious of meals, but it didn't hurt to eat that way every once in a while. She gave Gizmo one of his favorite dog treats, which he took to his bed in the living room.

Allison toyed with the idea of putting another movie in the player, but instead, she retrieved the first of Aunt Emma's journals from the bedroom. She wasn't going to get any work done this late in the day, so she might as well do something she enjoyed. She'd read a little of this first diary every night before turning out the light.

As Allison had expected, Aunt Emma had a way with written words, even at only fifteen. The stories in the journal—whether long or short—had captured Allison's imagination. She could easily envision the Carter family home back in the early twenties. And even though she'd seen many photographs of her grandmother, Elizabeth Carter Hendricks, there was something about Aunt Emma's descriptions that caused her to see her grandmother in a whole new way.

Before long, cheese and crackers were forgotten as Allison traveled back in time.

Emma

After returning from their honeymoon in New York City, Emma and Alexander rented a one-bedroom cottage in the north end of town. Her husband's job at the sawmill would never make them wealthy, but Emma was proud of how hard he worked and of the way she could make a dollar stretch. Still, she wondered sometimes if Alexander noticed all she'd done to make their house a home.

It was a warm Sunday in early September, and the family had gathered at Liza and John's house for a leisurely dinner after church. When J.J. began to fuss, Liza took him upstairs to her bedroom so she could nurse him. Emma followed after them.

The baby wouldn't eat at first. He seemed to prefer crying to nursing. He'd been that way since birth, and the strain of it showed on Liza's pretty features.

"Are you getting enough sleep?" Emma asked, sitting on the edge of the bed.

Her sister shrugged. "I never get a full night's sleep. Everyone tells me this won't last forever. That he'll grow out of it. But, Emma, it's like he's hungry all the time, even after he nurses. I've tried everything I've been told to try, and nothing seems to help."

Emma felt ashamed. She'd been so happy setting up house with Alexander she hadn't seen Liza very often over the summer. Not often enough to be of any help to her. Of course, Liza and John had servants to see to their needs and tend to their big house. Emma had no one but herself to clean and cook. She told herself she needn't feel guilty—but she did.

Tears slipped from Liza's eyes to trail slowly down her cheeks. "Maybe there is something wrong with me. Maybe it's my fault."

"Oh, sis. That isn't true." Emma stood, went to the rocking chair, and knelt beside it, placing her hand on her sister's knee. "It will get better. I'm sure it will."

Liza wiped away the tears with the back of her free hand. At that moment J.J. stopped fussing and latched onto his mother, suddenly ready to eat. The sisters exchanged a glance and laughed in unison, then they settled into a contented silence.

Emma watched the baby nurse and prayed that motherhood would arrive for her as quickly as it had for Liza. Alexander hadn't said he was eager for children. Not in so many words. But every man wanted a son to carry on the family name. And if she could give him a son, then maybe he would—

"Are you happy, Emma?"

She lifted her gaze to meet Liza's. "Yes."

"You didn't look happy just then."

"If you must know, I was wishing for a baby of my own."

"Are you sure Alexander is ready for the responsibility?"

Emma stiffened as she drew back from her sister. "What do you mean? He's as able to handle the responsibility as John is."

"I wasn't trying to insult him or you. It's just that Alexander has always seemed . . . I don't know, concerned with his own happiness first. Others come in a distant second."

Emma started to rise.

"Please don't go," Liza said. "I'm sorry. I enjoy your company, and we so seldom get to be together like this."

"Well . . ." Emma settled down again. "Be careful what you say."

"I will. But promise me something, Emma."

"What?"

"Don't let yourself forget that girl you used to be. The one who climbed trees and dreamed big dreams and seemed so fearless."

"Liza . . . ," she said in warning.

"Sometimes it seems as if she has faded into a ghost of herself and she's in danger of disappearing in an instant."

"You are talking gibberish."

Liza gave her head a slow shake, but finally answered, "If you say so, Emma."

Allison

Excitement churned in Allison's stomach as she parked her SUV in the short-term lot at the Boise Airport. It seemed an eternity since she'd seen her daughter, but now she was going to get to spend time with her for the next six or seven weeks. The company Meredith worked for had sent her back to Boise to oversee an important project, an assignment that would last until after the New Year.

The only way this visit could have been better was if Meredith could stay with her mother every night. But with the accident of the Leonard boy still fresh in Allison's mind, she'd insisted Meredith remain in the valley with Tony during the week and come up to the mountains for the weekends. That long drive to work every day wasn't worth the risk. But she would have her daughter with her for both Thanksgiving and Christmas, and they would get to ring in the New Year together. Knowing that was all ahead of her made her heart sing for joy.

Allison got out of the car and pressed the key fob to lock the door. She leaned into a bitter November wind as she hurried across the lanes outside the lower level of the airport. Once inside, she rode the escalator up to the waiting area. Her watch told her she had a little while before the plane was due to land, so rather than stand staring at the automatic glass doors leading out from the concourses, she sat in one of the chairs off to one side.

A short while later passengers spilled through the doorway.

Businessmen in suits carrying briefcases. A tired-looking mother with two small children dragging their own rolling suitcases. Several soldiers, male and female, in desert-brown fatigues, duffel bags in hand. The enthusiastic welcome for the military passengers brought a mist to Allison's eyes. She was a sucker for such scenes—in airports, on the evening news, wherever.

Blinking the tears away, she glanced at the arrival board. Meredith's plane had landed. She stood, feeling the excitement rising again. Then she saw Tony walking toward her and her stomach dropped. Allison hadn't seen her ex since she visited him in the hospital in September. He'd looked gray and tired then. His appearance today was improved. He looked . . . healthy.

"Good. I'm not too late to welcome her," he said as he stopped at her side.

"Her plane's landed." Allison glanced through the glass doors and back again. "I didn't know you'd be here."

"I've missed her too, Allie."

"I know, but . . ." *But I wanted her all to myself.*

"I was hoping we could go out to lunch, the three of us, before you go home."

"I don't know. Meredith's bound to be tired. It's a long flight from San Antonio. She left before six this morning." Allison felt as selfish as she sounded.

Tony smiled, not seeming to notice her moodiness. "She's young. She can take it."

Respond in love, her heart told her. But how could she? She didn't love him anymore. Only she knew it was Christian love she was to put into practice, not the romantic kind.

"Look!" Tony's grin widened. "There she is."

Allison turned toward the glass doors in time to see them open before Meredith. Oh my. She looked wonderful! Allison headed toward her daughter at the same time Meredith saw her.

Both of them grinned and laughed and were almost in tears as they embraced. Holding her daughter was the best thing Allison had felt in ages.

When they drew apart, Meredith moved immediately to repeat the embrace with her father. Allison knew then that Tony had been fully forgiven by their daughter. For the ways he'd failed Meredith. For his drinking. For walking out on Allison. For the divorce. For everything.

Even as Allison remembered that forgiveness was what she'd taught her daughter to do, she felt a twinge of resentment.

Meredith stepped back from Tony and looked toward Allison again. "I didn't expect to see you both here."

"I surprised your mother," Tony responded. "I wanted all of us to eat together before you head for the hills."

"I'd love that, Dad. I'm famished. I ate a little at four o'clock this morning, and all I've had to eat since then were some peanuts. There wasn't time for a sandwich when I changed planes."

The decision had been made. Allison tried to put her best face on. "Where to?" she asked Tony.

He named a popular Mexican restaurant—always Meredith's favorite kind of food. "We'll have missed the lunch rush. Shouldn't be crowded by the time we get there."

"Sounds good," Meredith said.

He held out his hand to take her roll-aboard. "Let's go get your checked luggage."

Allison followed in the rear, feeling like the proverbial third wheel.

Emma

1927

Emma was with Liza and John in the hospital when their six-month-old son passed away. Even though J.J. had been such a fussy baby from birth, Emma had never thought her infant nephew would die. How could he when so many people were faithfully praying for him? How could he when he was adored by aunt and parents and grandparents and friends of the family?

As the life left their baby son's body, John gathered Liza into his arms, and the two of them wept softly. A lump formed in Emma's throat. Tribulation caused some couples to pull apart, but Liza and John were drawing closer. It was as clear as if there were a visible cord holding them together. Lucky pair, to have each other so completely.

Emma remembered the day Liza had told her she was pregnant. She remembered thinking how everything good happened to her younger, prettier sister. She'd had to fight envy that day. And every month since her own wedding, every time Emma had discovered she *wasn't* pregnant, she'd found herself fighting envy of her sister again.

But she hadn't wished this loss on Liza. Not this.

John's parents arrived then. There was more hugging and crying. Next Emma and Liza's parents came, and the sorrow that filled the small hospital room became more than Emma could bear. After promising her sister she would come to her house the following day, she slipped out of the hospital room and headed for home.

Dusk had settled over Boise by that time, and everything around Emma—sky, buildings, sidewalks—seemed dim and gray. Fitting, under the circumstances.

When she turned the corner onto her street, she saw Alexander's 1913 Model T parked in front of the house. A flutter erupted in her chest and she quickened her steps. Her husband was always hungry when he got home from the mill, and he didn't like to wait to eat. But surely he would understand why she didn't have his supper ready tonight.

Tears returned. Unhappiness welled up inside of her. It shamed her to feel that way. She had no right to be unhappy. There were many greater sorrows to be borne, like the sorrow John and Liza were carrying today. Emma, on the other hand, was married to the man she loved. God had given her the desire of her heart.

If only Alexander loved me.

But she'd known that was how it was—on the day he proposed, on their wedding day, during their honeymoon, even in their marriage bed. He didn't love her, and she was afraid he never would.

Allison

Meredith thumbed through one of the scrapbooks, filled with old photographs that Allison had put together. "Mom, I never knew you were an artist. On the computer, yes. But not like this. When did you learn to scrapbook this way?"

"I took a class at the craft store a few summers ago."

"Too bad most people just take digital shots." Her daughter glanced up and shrugged. "Me included. I've got close to a thousand photos on my iPhone and will probably never do anything with them except stream them to my computer or add some of them to Facebook."

"I have a lot on my phone too."

Meredith closed the scrapbook. "Dad looks good. Didn't you think so? He must be feeling better."

Feeling better. Their mother-daughter code for *not drinking.*

"Maybe this time it'll stick," Meredith added.

"I hope so, honey." And Allison meant it. She really did. A woman didn't love a man for a quarter of a century and give birth to his child without caring in some small way about him, even after the marriage ended.

"It's going to feel a bit strange to stay in my old room without you being in the house too."

"Nothing I can do about that."

Meredith nodded, showing her acceptance. "You'd better show me where I'm staying so I can get organized."

Allison led the way up the stairs. She'd managed to change one of the bedrooms into something other than a glorified junk closet. She'd filled it with homey, feminine touches, from the pictures she'd hung on the walls to the dressing table with a matching stool to the decorative lamp and shade on the nightstand. A new bedspread covered the double-sized mattress. It was pale green, Meredith's favorite color.

"Mom, it's so pretty. Did you do this for me?"

"Of course."

Meredith turned and gave Allison a tight embrace. "I love you so much."

"I love you too," she whispered, choked by sudden emotion.

Her daughter drew back, her expression serious. "I wish I could have been with you this last year. I know it was harder on you than you admitted."

Allison nodded. "Sometimes it was." She smiled, driving away darker thoughts.

"We'll have a great time while I'm here, Mom. I'm looking forward to meeting all your new friends in Kings Meadow."

"That's good because I've invited a number of them to join us for Thanksgiving."

Meredith was silent for a short while before she asked, "What about Dad?"

"What about him?"

"He'll be alone for Thanksgiving."

Throughout her marriage to Tony, Allison had tried never to speak harshly of him to their daughter. She'd tried never to pretend there weren't problems, but she'd made certain never to make him a villain. Still, she wasn't ready to do what Meredith was asking. Asking without actually asking.

"Dad and I could have our Thanksgiving on Wednesday night, and then I could drive up on Thursday morning."

"That's a good idea." Her reply made Allison feel small and petty. For her daughter's sake, couldn't she—

No. There'd been one too many Thanksgiving dinners spoiled by Tony's behavior. She wasn't about to let this one be spoiled too. Not this year. This year she was making a new tradition in her new home with her new friends. Tony was her past. Allison was looking to the future. Meredith would have to accept that was how it must be.

"I'll leave you to get settled in," Allison said, taking a step backward. "Do you feel up to taking a walk with me and Gizmo before it gets dark?" She glanced at her watch. "We'd need to go soon. It gets dark fast."

"A walk would be great. I can unpack later. Let's go now."

Relief came in a rush, and only then did Allison realize she'd been afraid Meredith would be angry with her for refusing her request. Relief was followed by a surge of pride in the adult her daughter had become, despite the dysfunction in their home as she grew up.

"I'll need to borrow a warmer coat, Mom. My Texas jacket won't be anywhere near warm enough."

"I'll get one for you," Allison answered, then hurried down the stairs.

A short while later they set off down the driveway. Daylight was already waning, the sun having moved beyond the tall mountains to the west. Twigs and leaves snapped beneath their feet, but the weatherman promised it would snow again soon. And this time, Allison was convinced, the snow would stay on the ground until spring rolled around.

"Texas made me forget what real cold is," Meredith said as they crossed the road and descended the path to the river. "Brr."

"Colder than in the valley too."

Meredith looked across the river. "I always loved to come visit Aunt Emma when I was little. It's so pretty here."

Allison nodded. "Mmm."

"You seem really at home, Mom. More than I thought you would."

"More than *I* thought I would." Allison laughed softly, then drew in a deep breath and let it out, a frosty cloud forming before her mouth. "I'm grateful Aunt Emma left the house to me. I thought it would always be a vacation home for us, but now that I'm living here . . ." She shrugged as she let the sentence trail into silence.

"It surprised me that you let Dad have the house without a fight. At the time, I wanted him to suffer more. I thought you should take everything. Punish him. Leave him with nothing. I was so mad at him for what he did. Sometimes I still am."

Allison stopped walking and waited for Meredith to do the same. When her daughter turned to face her, Allison asked, "Was I wrong to stay with your father all those years? Did my decision to stay and keep on hoping cause you too much pain?"

"I didn't turn out too bad."

"No. Answer me, Meredith."

Her daughter looked across the river again. Her shoulders rose and fell on a sigh. "Who can say, Mom? I am who I am because of the past. Both good and bad. Maybe I'm stronger because of how things were when Dad was drinking. Maybe I'm messed up a little because of it too. But Dad wasn't all bad, even at his worst."

"I know."

"He could be a lot of fun."

"Yes, he could."

"And you loved him, Mom, despite everything."

"Yes, I loved him."

Meredith hooked arms with Allison. "I can tell you're going to turn out okay too. That's what matters to me now. That you're going to be okay."

June 1989

Allison put Meredith—belly full and sound asleep—into the cradle, then stood gazing down at her. A smile played across Allison's lips. She hadn't expected motherhood to make her feel like this. Thrilled and terrified at the same time.

"Hey, beautiful."

She turned to find Tony watching her from the bedroom doorway.

"Don't you need to get changed? Your mom's going to be here any minute and we have a reservation to get to."

"Are you sure we should go out tonight? What if Meredith wakes up and needs to be fed again?"

"She'll get by with a bottle for one evening. It's our anniversary, and we're going out."

"But—"

"I want to have a nice dinner with my wife and maybe dance with her a bit."

There was a smoldering look in his eyes that made her heart go all aflutter. He'd always had that effect on her. A glance. The brush of his finger along her forearm. His breath on her neck. It all left her weak in the knees.

The doorbell rang. "There's Grandma," Tony said, then disappeared from view.

Allison went to the closet and pulled out one of her favorite dresses. Would it fit? She was still packing a few baby pounds. Hoping for the best, she shed her top and shorts and put on the dress. She turned and looked at her reflection in the mirror. A relieved sigh escaped her. The dress looked pretty good, if she did say so herself.

"Knock, knock. May I come in?"

Allison turned toward the bedroom door as her mother entered the room, making a beeline toward the cradle. "Hi, Mom."

"How's our little angel?"

"Perfect. She just fell asleep a bit ago. With any luck she'll stay that way until we get home. But if she doesn't, there are a couple of bottles of breast milk in the refrigerator."

Her mother turned from the cradle to meet Allison's gaze. "I don't want you to worry about a thing. The baby and I will be just fine. You and Tony go and enjoy yourselves. Don't give us a single thought." She flicked her wrist at Allison, as if shooing her away. "Finish getting ready, darling. Your husband is waiting."

Happiness washed over Allison. A joy that was almost more than she could contain. She had the best parents, the best husband, the best baby in the world.

It just didn't get any better than this.

Emma

1927

The family gathered around the table in Roger and Pearl Carter's dining room on Thanksgiving Day, everyone doing their best to make it seem a festive affair. But it was hard, the loss of baby J.J. too recent to be forgotten, even for an hour or two. Emma saw the lingering sadness in her sister's eyes, and it made her own heart break. She also noticed how tenderly John spoke to his wife. She saw how tenderly he touched Liza, smiled at her, listened to her. And this, too, made her heart ache, though for a different reason.

There was an empty chair at the table next to Emma. Alexander hadn't yet joined them for dinner. He'd told Emma he had something to do and would get to his in-laws' home as soon as possible. Something to do on Thanksgiving? What could possibly be so urgent today?

Only she didn't have to ask that question. She knew the answer. It had something to do with what he did in his spare time. She wasn't supposed to know her husband was a bootlegger, but she did. And it frightened her. Frightened her to imagine what might happen to Alexander if he was caught by the authorities. Frightened her to know what kind of men—gangsters with guns!—he did business with. Frightened her because she knew things she wasn't supposed to know. And if she was foolish enough to reveal what she knew to Alexander or to ask him the wrong questions, she would make him angry. She could make him angry so easily. Especially if he'd been drinking some of that illegal alcohol himself. And he did drink it. He drank a lot of it.

It shamed her to admit it, but she was afraid of Alexander when he was angry. He'd never struck her, but there'd been times she thought he might. Sometimes she wanted to run away. But she loved him too much to leave, and it wasn't as if she hadn't known the man she'd chosen to marry. She'd seen his quick temper long before she'd become Mrs. Monroe. And she'd known he didn't love her even as he'd pledged himself to her.

"Emma?"

She met Liza's gaze across the table.

"Are you all right?" her sister asked softly.

She lied with a nod.

Did Liza believe her?

Please, God. Let her believe me.

Allison

The dining area in Allison's home was too small to hold everyone she'd invited for Thanksgiving dinner. So she'd borrowed a long table and folding chairs for the occasion, and Meredith set them up in the living room after she arrived from Boise on Thanksgiving morning. Their guests would include Susan and Ned Lyle; Chet and Marsha Leonard and their two teenage sons; and Pastor Josh Simpson, his wife, Becca, and their son, Tad.

Allison treasured the time she and Meredith had in the kitchen before their guests began to arrive. It was one of the great joys of life, she thought, the new relationship many mothers enjoyed with their daughters after they became adults. Meredith had gone through the normal pulling away during her teen years, but there hadn't been any ugly scenes of rebellion. Not like some families went through. By the time she graduated from college, a year sooner than most students her age, she'd blossomed into a beautiful, intelligent, strong-minded woman who loved God and had her feet firmly planted in reality. She'd also become her mother's dearest friend. Which had made her move to Texas especially hard on Allison.

But today they were together, and laughter filled the kitchen as they worked, Meredith peeling potatoes while Allison prepared the green bean casserole. Meredith must have inherited some of Aunt Emma's gift of gab. She shared funny stories from her job and the people she worked with and about her adjustment to Texas, especially the climate. She even shared about some disastrous dates she'd been on.

"I think I'm going to kiss dating good-bye, like the guy who wrote that book."

"You'll find someone," Allison said. "The right someone. I just wish he could be from Idaho, and you'd both move back."

"Not likely to happen while I'm living and working in San Antonio. Not many Idahoans living there that I've found."

"I know, but I can wish it, can't I?"

Meredith rinsed the last potato in the sink. "Wish away, Mom. I wouldn't mind coming home to Idaho for good, but I can't see the company transferring me back anytime soon."

Allison made a mental note to double her prayers for just that thing to happen.

The first of their guests arrived shortly after one o'clock— Pastor and Mrs. Simpson and their son with the Lyles close on their heels. It was more than half an hour later before Chet Leonard arrived with his two sons, sans Marsha.

"She wasn't feeling up to being with other people today," he said, explaining his wife's absence.

"I'm sorry to hear it." Allison took his hat and coat. "I'll send a plate home with you so she doesn't miss out on the Thanksgiving meal."

"That's really kind."

She didn't offer him any advice. She didn't know him all that well. But perhaps she could find some way to encourage Marsha, woman to woman. She and Susan could put their heads together and come up with some ideas. With a nod, she turned and carried the collected coats and Chet's hat into her bedroom.

Allison and her company sat at the table at two o'clock. The pastor blessed the food, and then everyone passed the serving dishes until their own plates were piled high. Roast turkey and stuffing. Mashed potatoes and gravy and hot, buttered rolls. Green beans and sweet potatoes and peas with pearl onions. Olives and pickles, celery and carrots.

It was over coffee and dessert—apple pie with ice cream or pumpkin pie with whipped cream or some of both—when conversations melded together and turned not to the holiday of Thanksgiving but to thanking the Giver of all. Allison wasn't sure who started it, but soon they were going around the table, one by one, naming people and things they were thankful for.

First came the expected: Thankful for my husband. Thankful for my wife. Thankful for my children. Thankful for my health.

But eventually someone spoke the unexpected.

"I'm thankful God didn't answer my prayer about a job I wanted my first year out of college." Chet tipped his chair onto its back legs. "Would've made a lot of money, but we wouldn't have had the life we were supposed to have. Our children wouldn't have grown up in such a tight community, learning the values I want them to have. I'm thankful God said no to something good so we could have something better." His voice softened. "I'm especially glad Rick got to grow up the way he did."

Everyone seemed to hold their breaths at the mention of his son. Empathy tightened Allison's chest. How hard it was to speak of the loved one who was no longer present. Especially at first.

"I nursed my mother for a few years before she died," Becca Simpson said, breaking the silence at long last. "She had dementia. It was hard to watch her fail that way. But I've never known the Lord to be so close as He was in those years. I'm thankful to Him for that dark valley of testing because it brought me closer to our Savior."

Others continued in that vein, but Allison no longer listened.

Am I thankful for the hard things and disappointments that have happened in my life? The question made her uncomfortable—because she wanted to answer in the affirmative but she couldn't.

Allison

The house felt empty, almost abandoned, after Meredith drove back to Boise on Sunday afternoon. After four days and three nights with her daughter's constant company, Allison wasn't sure what to do with herself in the midst of the silence. She thought about starting another of her aunt's journals. Or she could work on her latest scrapbook of old photographs. Neither choice beckoned to her.

With a mug of decaf in hand, she settled at last into a favorite chair in the living room and stared at the flames in the fireplace. Before she could take her first sip of coffee, the telephone rang. The call was from Susan.

"I thought you'd be feeling at loose ends with Meredith gone again," her friend said after they'd greeted each other.

"You know me well."

"Friday will be here before you know it."

"Maybe that's the real problem. January will be here before I know it too, and Meredith will go back to Texas."

"Let tomorrow take care of itself. Each day has enough trouble of its own."

She nodded, as if Susan could see her. Her friend was offering good—and scriptural—advice. If only knowing and doing were the same thing.

Susan must have decided it was time to change the subject

before Allison found herself in tears. "Have you had time to start reading our book for December's book club?"

"Not yet. I'm not sure I'm up for something that takes deep thought. I usually enjoy biographies and memoirs, but I don't know about this one. It's going to be so sad. I can tell from the back cover blurb. A humorous novel would have suited me better."

"You'll get your turn to pick what you like."

"I know. But to tell you the truth, I'd rather read Aunt Emma's journals. I love getting a glimpse into her life when she was a teenager. Things were so different back then, and yet they were a lot the same. Times change but people don't. Not really."

"Maybe you should think about publishing Emma's journals."

"All of them?"

Susan laughed. "Of course not. But I'll bet you could pick and choose from the entries. Just the right ones to let readers catch a glimpse of her life. The rest of the book could be of your favorite photographs she took. You could include some of her more famous ones and then some of the more obscure."

"Interesting thought."

"It's more than interesting. It's a good idea. A really good idea. You should do it."

"Okay. Okay. I promise to think about it. I've got a lot of journals to read before I'll know if there's anything I could do with them."

"You be sure you do think about it. Hey, listen. I've got to run. Ned's calling me."

"Okay. Talk to you later."

"Later," Susan echoed. Then the connection was gone.

Allison's coffee had grown cold while she talked to her friend. She carried the mug into the kitchen and put it in the microwave for thirty seconds.

Publish a book about her aunt? It was a rather outlandish idea. Allison wasn't a writer by any stretch of the imagination. Although she had to admit, reading Aunt Emma's journals had given her the desire to keep one of her own. Maybe now would be a good time to make that first entry.

She went into the bedroom, retrieved her Bible along with some highlighters, a pen, and a spiral-bound journal she'd recently purchased, and carried everything to the kitchen table.

But where to begin?

She took a sip of coffee from her mug, opened the journal, and began to write.

Just who is Allison Marie Knight Kavanagh?

It's embarrassing to reach the age of 45 and not have a quick and easy answer to the question. As a child, I was the beloved daughter and pesky little sister. In my twenties and thirties I was a wife and mother.

But somewhere along the way, I think I lost track of me.

No, not somewhere. It happened when I tried to become Tony's savior instead of his wife. I wasn't very good at that. I tried to be his rock. Wasn't good at that either. When did I start believing that was the role God wanted me to play in our marriage? When did I become so desperate to hold all the tattered pieces together instead of learning to trust, instead of leaning into Jesus?

A good Christian isn't supposed to get divorced. That's what people say. That's what I've always believed. And yet here I am. Divorced. Maybe I'm not a good Christian.

Even as she wrote the last sentences, she knew they were wrong. Not that she wasn't supposed to live in obedience to God, but that she was supposed to live under grace rather than by her works. The gospel itself wasn't complicated, but sometimes being a disciple of Christ was. Following rules, she'd found, was—or seemed to be—easier than walking by faith and listening to the Spirit. So much easier to believe that if she did X Y Z, then A B C would happen.

Just who is Allison Marie Knight Kavanagh today? I need to find out. I need God to reveal my identity to me.

And what about that conversation everyone had on Thanksgiving? The one about thanking God for hard things in our lives. God walked with me after Tony left and He was there when I was grieving over my failed marriage. He was there even when I didn't talk to Him or acknowledge Him. But am I grateful for what He taught me in those horrible months? Is it possible not to want to be divorced and yet be able to thank God in the midst of it? Or even for it? I think it must be. The Bible says so. But how do I learn to do it?

Allison laid down the pen and rubbed her forehead with her fingertips. Introspection wasn't easy or particularly fun. But if it would draw her closer to God, she wanted to keep going. She picked up the pen again.

When I moved into Aunt Emma's house, I felt far from the Lord. It isn't that way anymore. But I don't want to settle for just knowing He is near. I can't put into words what I do want, but I don't want only the status quo. Savior and Lord. Jesus wants to be both in my life. I don't doubt I'm saved and going to heaven. But have I let Him be Lord over every area of my life?

An uncomfortable question. Perhaps one too many for this first attempt at putting her feelings on paper. She set down the pen a second time and rose from her chair. Full darkness had arrived while she was at the table in the kitchen, and although it was still early—not even six thirty—she was ready to turn in.

Emma

1928

Alexander rolled his truck off the road on a cold February night. He was taken to the hospital where a doctor set his broken left leg and stitched the wounds under his right eye and on both arms. He was in a bed in one of the wards by the time Emma arrived, her heart pumping with fear.

It shamed her, the relief she felt when she saw him in that narrow hospital bed with his leg in a cast and his eyes closed. Not because he would be all right, given time to heal, but because, for at least a few weeks, he would be immobile. In her mind that was a good thing, despite the lost income. He would be in less danger from the law—and from the men he worked for—as long as he was confined to their home.

She moved to the side of the bed and touched his shoulder. "Alexander?"

He opened his eyes.

"I came as soon as I heard." She sank onto a metal chair. "The nurse told me you won't be able to work for six weeks but that you'll make a full recovery as long as you do as you're told."

His cheek twitched, a telltale sign of simmering anger.

"Are you in much pain?"

"It hurts plenty." He scowled at her. "You need to find out what happened to the truck. If I don't have it"—he glanced around, making certain no one was eavesdropping—"I'll fall behind in my deliveries."

"You can't drive with your leg in a cast."

"No, but you can drive. I'll just tell you where to go."

"Alexander, I've barely learned how to drive. I can't—"

"You'll do what I tell you to do, Emma."

She dropped her voice to a whisper as she leaned in. "I can't do it. It's wrong."

"I'll get out of this bed and show you what's wrong."

Before she could react, he grabbed a handful of her hair and yanked her to him, so close their cheeks almost touched. His lips were near her ear.

"If you want a roof over your head and food to eat, woman, you'll do as you're told."

Tears welled in her eyes. When had Alexander become this man? When had he become this cruel? When had his tongue become so sharp? Had she only imagined his sense of humor and his good-natured teasing? Had she only pretended he liked her? Before they were married, they'd been friends. Hadn't they?

He released her hair. "Stop your sniveling, Emma. It's me who got hurt. I'm your husband, and you'll do what I say."

She'd wanted to marry Alexander. More than anything else, she'd wanted it. God had given her what she'd asked for, what she'd been willing to do anything to get, but it had come at a price.

As her mother had warned on many occasions, she'd made her bed and now she had to lie in it. That was just the way things were.

Allison

Winter came to the mountains with a vengeance. Beginning in December, Allison hired a man to plow her driveway whenever there was fresh snowfall, and soon there was a wall of white over six feet high on either side of the narrow drive.

On the Sunday before Christmas, Allison and Meredith were able to make it into Kings Meadow to attend church, then returned home for lunch and a couple hours of conversation before Meredith planned to head down to Boise for the work week.

Not long before Meredith was set to leave, she popped an unexpected question: "Can Dad join us for Christmas?"

"Oh, Meredith."

"I understand why you said no for Thanksgiving. You had all those people coming over. But Christmas, it's just you and me. What can it hurt to let him be here? He's all alone, Mom. He doesn't have any family but us."

Us? A selfish part of Allison wanted to keep Meredith all to herself. In that petty corner of her heart, she could admit she'd liked it when Meredith was angry with her father and not speaking to him. But their father-daughter relationship seemed to have mended, and now Allison had to share Meredith again. Either her daughter's time must be divided between her parents or her parents must see her at the same time. Those were the only two choices.

"Would it be all right if he drove up here with me on Friday? Then he and I can go back together on Monday."

Allison felt her eyes go wide. "You want your dad to stay here for three days?"

"Sure. Why not? Mom, it would be fun. You remember the good times we used to have up here as a family."

But we're not a family anymore. By his *choice!* "Where would he sleep?"

"He could have my bed and I'll take the couch."

"Meredith . . ."

"Or Dad can buy one of those blow-up beds and bring it with him. Those things are pretty decent. I've slept on one before."

Allison felt the resistance drain out of her. Almost from birth, Meredith had had the ability to twist her mother around her little finger. A pleading smile, and Allison was putty in her hands.

"Please say yes, Mom. It's Christmas. I won't be in Idaho much longer."

Exactly the reason I want you to myself. She released a sigh. "All right. He can come if he wants to. But if he . . . if he doesn't *behave,* he'll have to leave."

Meredith threw her arms around Allison and gave her a tight squeeze. "Thanks, Mom. And don't worry about Dad. He's doing good. He really is. He's sober and working his program. Did I tell you I went with him to an open meeting last week?"

"What?" Allison drew back, stunned by that bit of information.

"Yeah, I did. It was kind of interesting, really. Dad spoke some. I was proud of him. You'll be proud of him too. You'll see. Have a little faith. Believe in him."

Allison had believed in Tony one time too many, just to have her hopes dashed again. Three months ago Meredith had called her in a panic because her dad was in the hospital. Again. Because of his drinking. Again. And now she wanted him to come stay in her mother's home for Christmas.

It was a lot to ask.

It was too much to ask.

Through the years Allison had known other couples who'd divorced. When there were children involved, there'd been difficult dynamics, especially around birthdays and holidays. But she'd thought those difficulties were restricted to the divorced parents of school-aged children. How naive she'd been. She hadn't known the dynamics were still difficult when the children were adults.

Well, she couldn't change her mind now. She'd already agreed to let Tony come.

Meredith was all smiles as she put her luggage into the rental car and then bid her mother good-bye. From the deck, Allison watched until the car turned onto the highway and disappeared from view.

What have I done?

"Come on, Gizmo. Let's go inside where it's warm."

Not a fan of snow, the dog was quick to obey.

Allison stopped inside the doorway as memories washed over her. Memories of her and Tony and Meredith staying at Aunt Emma's house, hiking in the mountains, rafting the river. They'd made many good memories here. Many of them. But bad memories seemed to rise to the top. Why was that? Bad ones supplanted the good ones until it seemed they'd all been bad.

Odd, wasn't it? She'd spent a lot of years trying not to see what was going on because she didn't know how to deal with it, pretending everything in her life was okay. Now it seemed she wanted to believe everything in her old life had been sour and spoiled. But the truth was somewhere in the middle.

Releasing a sigh, she went upstairs and looked into the guest room. Her daughter had left it as neat as a pin. Once upon a time—not all that long ago—Meredith's bedroom had looked like a cyclone blew through it.

An image of Tony sleeping in the guest room bed flooded Allison's mind. An unsettling image. It hadn't been fair of Meredith to ask her to let him come stay for Christmas. Allison was making a new life for herself. Seeing Tony just brought up a lot of bad feelings.

But she knew that come Friday evening, he would be her houseguest. He wouldn't be able to refuse Meredith either. For all the negative things Allison might say about her ex-husband, a lack of love for his daughter wasn't one of them. Not that he'd always shown his love in the best of ways. Still . . .

She stepped backward out of the room, then moved to the second upstairs bedroom. Officially, it was her exercise room, complete with treadmill, yoga mat, and television with DVD player. Unofficially, it stored everything she hadn't decided what to do with yet. If she shoved some boxes around, she might be able to make room in it for a queen-sized blow-up mattress. Meredith shouldn't have to give up her bed.

Resentment rushed back. Resentment for years of hurts and embarrassments and medical bills and dashed hopes and destroyed dreams and, finally, a failed marriage. Even resentment for the resentment. Setting her jaw, she tried to force the feeling away. She'd been doing so much better. She didn't want to slide into melancholy or anger again.

Three nights wouldn't be so bad. She could handle it. She *would* handle it. Starting right now.

Allison

Allison was looking out the living room window when Meredith's rental car returned on Friday. More snow had fallen during the week, and the wall of white on either side of the driveway had grown another six to eight inches. It was truly a winter wonderland.

Allison grabbed her warmest coat from the rack and went outside to welcome them. "How were the roads?" she called when Meredith stepped out from the driver's side.

"Good. They're mostly dry."

Allison's gaze shifted to the passenger side as Tony exited the vehicle.

"Merry Christmas, Allie," he said, sounding somewhat hesitant. Was he as unsure about the days to come as she was?

"Merry Christmas, Tony." She forced a smile and hoped it looked genuine. "You and Meredith get your stuff and come in from the cold."

She should have gone down the steps and helped, but nervous energy sent her back inside. She went straight to the kitchen and busied herself making hot chocolate with marshmallows floating in the froth on top. A little thumping and banging from above told her Meredith and her dad were settling in to their rooms. Allison put the hot beverages on a tray and carried it up the stairs. Father and daughter were in the exercise room, inflating a queen-sized air mattress with a small electric pump.

"How about some hot chocolate, you two?" she said above the noise.

The blower switched off, plunging the room into silence.

"That sounds good, Mom." Still on her knees, Meredith twisted around and reached to take one of the mugs.

"Tony?"

"You bet. I'd love one."

Allison took the last mug in her left hand and leaned the tray against the wall outside the room. All three were silent as each blew across the surface of their hot beverages and tried to take their first sips without burning their tongues.

It was Meredith who spoke first. "You did more decorating this week, Mom."

"Some."

"Everything looks pretty and festive. The tree makes the whole house smell good." Meredith looked at her dad. "Mom and I got the tree and decorated it last Saturday, but she's done everything else while I was in Boise."

Tony frowned as he placed a hand on Meredith's shoulder. "I didn't do anything. I didn't even put up a tree for you, kid. Sorry."

"It's okay, Dad. We all knew I was spending Christmas with Mom."

"Yeah, but still . . ." He shrugged.

Meredith took another few sips of the hot chocolate, then set the mug aside and turned the blower back on. No one tried to speak above the noise. Allison stood there a short while longer. Then, feeling unnecessary, she turned and went downstairs.

Burning wood crackled and popped in the fireplace while Christmas music came through speakers in two corners of the living room. The Douglas fir, set to one side of the picture

window, sparkled with multicolored mini-lights. Ornaments—
many of them with special meaning from Meredith's childhood
as well as from Allison's own childhood—covered the tree from
top to bottom.

Allison loved the Christmas season. She had since she was a
little girl. She loved the excitement and anticipation. She loved
finding the perfect gift for each person on her shopping list. She
loved the carolers and the Christmas pageants and the houses
covered in lights.

She smiled, remembering what their home in Boise had
looked like every year from Thanksgiving through New Year.
Tony, a homeowner with a competitive spirit, had started many
years ago with a few strings of lights along the roofline. But every
time another homeowner in the neighborhood did something
more, he would have to one-up them in return. Sometimes the
same year. Sometimes the next.

Her smile faded, replaced by a sting of sadness at the knowledge Tony hadn't strung a single strand of lights this year. Had
she been the reason he'd done it in the past? Was he content to
have it the way it was now?

She moved closer to the tree and fingered a few of the ornaments. The one of Santa on a dolphin had come from Disney
World the year Meredith was ten. The cowboy Santa came from
a trip Allison had taken to Cheyenne. The Scarlett O'Hara and
Rhett Butler ornaments had been a gift from her mother because
she and Allison both loved the movie—and book—so much. As
had Aunt Emma.

Tears sprang to Allison's eyes. Hearing footsteps on the
stairs, she quickly blinked them away. Then, drawing a deep
breath to steady herself, she turned around.

Tony stopped on the bottom step. He looked good. Healthy.
Different from the last few times she'd seen him. Meredith had

said her dad was back on the wagon, and from his appearance, Allison believed it. But would it last? It had only been three months since his drinking had put him in the hospital.

When Allison was a teenager, the pastor of the church she'd attended with her parents had shared his personal story of alcoholism. As he told it, on the day he'd found faith in Jesus, all desire to drink vanished in an instant. A miracle, he'd called it. But for some reason it was a miracle she'd *expected* when she discovered Tony's problem. It had taken years and many disappointments for her to come to a place of understanding that miracles were miracles because they were rare. Most often in the trials of life, Jesus said, "Be yoked with Me, and we'll walk through this together."

She'd wanted the miracle. Why hadn't God given her the miracle?

"What's the plan, Mom?"

Pulled from her unsettled thoughts by her daughter's question, Allison blinked. "I . . . I'm not sure. What would you like to do?" She glanced at the clock. "We won't have supper for another hour."

"How about watching *A Christmas Carol*? The one with Alastair Sim. You've still got that DVD, don't you?"

"Yes, I have it."

"And after we eat, we can watch *A Christmas Story*. I know you must have that one too. I bought my own copy last year."

It was all a bit surreal, having a family Christmas when they were no longer a family. Last year she and Tony had been living apart, but she'd still hoped for reconciliation. As for all of the Christmases before that . . .

She pointed toward the carousel that held her collection of movie disks. "They're alphabetical by title."

"Mom!" Laughing, Meredith rolled her eyes. "Do you think I don't know that about you?"

Tony smiled too, but Allison could see he was as nervous and unsure as she was.

She hoped they would make it through the next three days without suffering a disaster of one kind or another.

Emma

1928

Liza set a basket of groceries on the table before turning a stern gaze on her sister. "Are you feeling all right, Emma?"

"I'm fine. Just tired. I haven't slept well since Alexander's accident."

"You would tell me if it was more than that, wouldn't you?"

Emma shrugged. "Of course."

"You're much too thin."

"That's the pot calling the kettle black."

Liza flashed a brief smile.

Emma pointed at the basket. "You didn't need to bring food."

"With Alexander not bringing in a paycheck? Of course we're going to help. John and I are your family."

Pride wanted her to refuse, but Liza was right. They did need the help. "Can you stay for a cup of tea?"

"I'd love one." Liza pulled a chair out from the table and sat on it. "Where's Alexander? In the bedroom?"

"No. One of his friends took him somewhere."

"When does he go back to work at the sawmill?"

"Next week." Emma filled the kettle with water and set it on the stove to heat. "It will be good for him. He's bored to tears sitting around the house all the time."

Liza played with the hem of her sweater, her eyes fixed on Emma. "Does he ever . . . take out his boredom . . . on you?"

Emma wanted to die. She wanted to sink right through the floor and disappear. Never ever ever did she want anyone—and especially not her beautiful sister with the perfect marriage—to guess that Alexander didn't love her. Had never loved her. Could be so cruel with his words that sometimes she felt threatened. It was too shameful a thing.

"Em?"

She sucked in air through her nose and met her sister's gaze with determination. "I don't know what you mean, Liza."

"Don't you? Sometimes, he seems so . . . so—"

"We're every bit as happy together as you and John."

"You've changed too, Emma. You're like a shadow of the girl you used to be."

Liza's words stung. Emma wanted to deny them, but the protest caught in her throat.

The water began to boil, and Emma was glad for a reason to turn away, afraid her expression would reveal too much. Her hands shook as she prepared the tea. When it was ready, Emma joined Liza at the table. They sipped the hot beverage in awkward silence for several minutes.

Finally, Liza set her tea cup on the table. "There's something I came to tell you."

At this point Emma wasn't sure she wanted to hear anything from Liza. It would be better if she left. Now. Before Alexander returned. Before—

"I'm pregnant again, Em."

Her heart stopped beating at the news.

"The baby's due in the autumn."

Emma drew a quick breath and forced herself to speak. "That . . . that's wonderful, Liza. John must be over the moon."

"He is. We both are." Tears welled in Liza's eyes, and her voice dropped to a whisper. "The house has felt terribly empty since

J.J. died. I know we can't replace one child with another. J.J. will always be our firstborn. We will always love him. But still . . ." Her words trailed into another silence.

Emma felt the emptiness of her womb like a knife through the heart. She wanted a baby. She wanted Alexander's baby. If she could give him a son, then maybe—

"It will happen for you too," Liza said, seeming to read Emma's thoughts. "Just give it time."

"Will it? You got pregnant on your honeymoon. We've been married nine months already."

"Maybe God is telling you to wait awhile. Maybe you and Alexander need this time for just the two of you before you start a family."

Emma almost laughed aloud at Liza's comment. She didn't think her husband enjoyed being with her. So much of the time he was angry, discontented, resentful—and he blamed her for his unhappiness. She'd tried hard to be the kind of wife he wanted, but there was one thing about herself she couldn't change no matter how hard she tried.

She could never become Liza.

Allison

It was close to eleven by the time the credits began to roll at the end of *A Christmas Story*.

Meredith punched Stop on the remote, then rose from the floor in front of the sofa and stretched her arms high above her head, releasing a soft groan. "I think it's time for bed."

"I think you're right," Allison answered.

Meredith leaned down and kissed Allison on the cheek, then repeated the action with her father who was seated in a nearby chair. "Good night, you two. See you in the morning."

Allison watched their daughter climb the stairs and disappear into the guest bedroom. Oh, how she would miss her when she returned to Texas. The days were speeding by so fast.

"Allie?"

She looked toward Tony. His face was cast in shadows, most of the light in the room coming from the Christmas tree and the television.

"Thanks for letting me come."

"I did it for Meredith." Ungracious words, but she couldn't help them.

"I understand. I appreciate it anyway."

"I suppose as long as she lives in Texas, we'll have to get used to spending time together whenever she visits."

"Allie, can I tell you I'm sorry?"

"Sorry? For what?"

"For everything I've done to hurt you or make you unhappy."

That covers a lot of ground.

"It wasn't what I wanted to do."

Allison was too tired to have this conversation. And what good would it do? They were divorced. She'd had to let go of him. If not for their daughter she'd likely never have seen him again.

"I'm trying to get my life back together again, Allie. It isn't easy. I've mucked it up plenty. Nobody knows that better than you. But I'm trying to make amends wherever I can."

Make amends. Familiar jargon of twelve-step groups everywhere. How does anyone make amends for throwing away years and years? Not just years of his own life but years of the people who loved him. It couldn't be done. He was too late. At one time she'd believed it could happen. She didn't believe it anymore.

"Maybe now isn't the time," Tony said softly, "but I hope you'll let me talk to you sometime about what's happened with me. It's important."

Allison stood. "Sure. Sometime. But not now. I'm going to bed. Good night, Tony. Turn off the tree lights before you turn in, will you?"

"Yes. I will."

She escaped the discomfort of the living room, Gizmo following on her heels. Her thoughts whirled as she completed her bedtime routine—washing and moisturizing her face, brushing and flossing her teeth, swallowing her calcium and magnesium supplements, putting on her long-sleeved nightshirt. After crawling into bed, snuggling beneath the warm comforter, she grabbed her Kindle, knowing she wouldn't fall asleep right away. Not until she stopped feeling agitated.

She wasn't certain how many pages she'd read before realizing not a single word had made sense to her. She hadn't a clue what was happening in the novel. A groan rumbled in her chest as she closed the leather cover and set aside the electronic reader.

God, what's wrong with me? I can't make sense of what I'm feeling.

All in all, it had been a pleasant evening. Conversation at supper had been congenial, most of it centered on Meredith and her job and her friends in Texas. It had been fun to watch their two most favorite Christmas movies together. It hadn't felt nearly as strange as Allison had feared it might. Right up until Tony's "I'm sorry" it had been all right.

"Allie, can I tell you I'm sorry?"

It was too late for sorry. Much too late. Of all people, Tony ought to understand that.

She closed her eyes, willing her thoughts to grow still, willing her body to let her escape into sleep. And willing herself not to remember. Not the good. Not the bad.

But her mind didn't obey.

She dreamed they were young again. Young and poor and happy. She dreamed of their first apartment, of the fun they had, buying used furniture and hanging cheap reproductions on the walls of the three small rooms. She dreamed of the laughter they shared and of the way he held her at night in their double bed. She dreamed of a time when she hadn't been afraid of what tomorrow would bring.

July 1993

Allison was still smiling as she turned the car onto Mountain View Drive. She and several friends—two of whom had been bridesmaids at her wedding—had spent the evening watching the Idaho Shakespeare Festival's production of *The Comedy of Errors*. Delightful from start to finish. Worth getting home so late, even though Meredith would have Allison up early tomorrow morning. Meredith rarely slept beyond 6:00 a.m.

As she approached the house, she pressed the button on the garage remote. The door was open by the time she pulled into the driveway. The outside lights hadn't been turned on, despite Allison's having reminded Tony to do so as she was leaving.

Irritation tightened the set of her mouth. But then her headlights hit the door leading into the house. First, she saw it was ajar. Then she saw a leg and foot in the opening. Panicked, she braked, killed the engine, and got out of the car in a matter of seconds.

"Tony? Tony?" She rushed to the door, opened it all the way, and stepped over her husband. "Tony?" She knelt near his head. "What happened? What's wrong?" Should she call for an ambulance? He was too young for a heart attack. Wasn't he?

He groaned.

Thank heaven. He wasn't dead.

And then she smelled it. Alcohol. He reeked of it.

She rocked backward, off her knees and onto her fanny, her back against the wall.

How long had he been out? How had he ended up like this, half in and half out of the house? Where was Meredith?

Meredith!

Allison was on her feet in an instant and running toward her daughter's bedroom. She pushed open the door, and the hall light spilled into the room and onto the twin-sized bed. Four-year-old Meredith was sound asleep, the sheet and blanket already down on the floor. Allison went to the bed and leaned over to brush dark curls off Meredith's forehead. Her heart rate slowed a little, knowing her daughter was unharmed. But what if—

She sank onto the floor a second time and let the tears come as she hugged her knees to her chest.

She'd known something was wrong. For weeks now she'd known. Maybe for months. But she hadn't let herself imagine Tony was drinking so much that he would pass out. Or that he would do it while he was in charge of Meredith. What had he been thinking? What was wrong with him?

O God, help us!

Allison

Allison awoke on Saturday morning to the smell of coffee wafting under her closed bedroom door. Beyond the blinds it was still dark. Christmas Eve.

She heard the rumble of Tony's deep voice followed by Meredith's lighter laughter. Father and daughter in the kitchen together. Allison wished she felt like laughing along with them, but she didn't. Although she'd slept through the night, her dreams had left her feeling drained. Definitely not in the holiday spirit.

Coffee would have to wait. First she needed to stand beneath a spray of hot water while she tried to put her emotions together.

By the time Allison was showered, her hair dried, makeup on, and dressed in comfy clothes, her daughter had prepared scrambled eggs, sausage links, and cinnamon rolls.

"Morning, sleepyhead," Meredith greeted her as she entered the kitchen. "OJ or grapefruit juice?"

"Grapefruit, please." Allison's gaze shifted to Tony, who was leaning a shoulder against the far wall. He looked relaxed, at ease, as if he belonged here. Which he didn't. "Morning, Tony."

"Morning."

Meredith retrieved the juice from the refrigerator and filled three small glasses to the brim.

"Can I help with anything?" Allison asked.

"No, we've got it, Mom. Everything's ready. Sit down and we'll all eat. I'm starved."

Tony pushed himself off the wall. "Me too." He joined them at the table.

"I'll say the blessing," Meredith said.

Allison bowed her head and closed her eyes.

"Dear Lord, thank You for bringing us all together this Christmas weekend. Thank You that we can celebrate Your birth. Help us follow Your lead today and tomorrow and every day thereafter. In Your name, we pray. Amen."

"Amen."

"Amen."

Allison looked up and gave Meredith a smile. There were many, many mistakes Allison had made in her life, but there sat living proof she'd done a few things right. Meredith hadn't lost her faith while in college the way so many young folks did. Instead, it had deepened. Allison liked to think she'd played at least a small part in that.

"Remember when I was little," Meredith said, "how hard it was for me to wait to open presents until after we ate breakfast?"

"I remember," Allison and Tony answered in unison.

"I thought you must be the meanest parents in the world, to make me wait like that."

"Funny," Tony broke in. "I remember more than one Christmas when your mom and I ate breakfast around four or five in the morning. Just so you could open your presents."

Meredith laughed. "True. I guess you did at that."

"I hope we won't be up that early tomorrow," he said.

"Oh, Dad, I'm past that phase. I'll let you sleep in at least until six."

More laughter filled the room.

What was that phrase people used? *Welcome to the new normal.* That was it. A new normal. Life changed all the time. No matter how hard one tried to keep things the same, one never succeeded. Children grew up. Jobs got outsourced. Husbands walked out on their wives. Summer became autumn. Autumn became winter. Parents passed away. The Bible said there was an appointed time for everything and a time for every purpose under heaven. There were many new normals to be experienced in life. This was one of Allison's.

The melody from one of her mother's favorite songs from the sixties played in her head. *Turn. Turn. Turn.* She smiled at the memory, picturing her mother playing the old vinyl record and singing along to it. Then Allison looked at Tony and Meredith again.

This was still her family, fractured though it was. This was her new normal. There was a time even for this under God's heaven.

In the afternoon the three of them strapped on snowshoes and traipsed off through the forest. Gizmo got to ride in a pet sling strapped to Allison's chest.

"Lucky dog," Meredith said, punctuating her words with a roll of the eyes.

After fifteen minutes of walking, they all needed to stop to peel off one layer of winter attire.

"When was the last time we went snowshoeing?" Tony asked, huffing the question.

"At least a decade." Allison shook her head. "I'm glad Aunt Emma kept the snowshoes, even if they weren't being used. They must be forty or fifty years old."

"Older, I bet."

They continued on, Meredith leading the way, Allison bringing up the rear. Sunlight filtered through the tall, lodgepole pines and reflected off the snow, blindingly bright. Thank goodness for sunglasses.

Watching the two people ahead of her, the song made famous by the Byrds returned to Allison's thoughts. *Turn. Turn. Turn.*

Last Christmas she'd been in a pit of despair about her failing marriage, about her life, about her shaky faith. She'd felt a complete failure in every realm. It surprised her to realize how far she'd come since then. It surprised her even more to realize how far she'd come since awakening this morning. What was different? She couldn't say. But something had changed.

Turn. Turn. Turn.

Acceptance, perhaps. Maybe a willingness, as they said in recovery programs, to let go and let God.

Aunt Emma had told her once that as long as a person was drawing breath, she could be certain God had a reason for leaving her on earth. Nobody's life was meaningless. The good Lord had a purpose and a plan for everyone.

On this Christmas Eve, Allison felt herself begin to believe her aunt's comments.

I'm still drawing breath, Lord. You've still got a purpose and a plan for me. Tell Aunt Emma I'm learning that lesson.

"Come on, Mom." Meredith's voice broke through Allison's musings. "You're falling behind. Hurry up."

"I'm coming! Hold your horses."

Emma

June 9, 1928

Today is our first anniversary. Strange. There are times it feels I've been married to Alexander forever, and other times when it seems only yesterday since we were pronounced man and wife.

We are almost happy, I think. Happier than we were when Alexander was in that cast and unable to get around easily. His mood is much improved. He doesn't seem as angry as before. The house seems more at peace. I don't think he's drinking as much as he used to. Sometimes I am hopeful he will learn to love me. Love me the way John loves Liza. And even if not that much, at least enough.

One thing weighs heavy on my heart, however. Alexander goes out every night. His bootlegging business has grown to include a couple of speakeasies. He doesn't need my help any longer, for which I am grateful. But if he is discovered in his nighttime activities he would go to jail. I would pray for God's protection, but how can I when what he is doing is against the law? I dare not say anything to him about my fears. He wouldn't listen, and it would make him angry. I do not want to make him angry again.

Tonight my parents are having us over for dinner in celebration of our anniversary. John and Liza will be there. Alexander does not want to go. He says my parents do not like him. No matter how often I tell him that is not true, he still believes it. He says they compare him to John and they think he comes up wanting.

Perhaps if I could give Alexander a child, he would feel better about himself (and about me). But another month has come around, and I am not pregnant. I want a baby so much. I watch my sister growing larger and larger with her second child. I know she is counting down the weeks until her baby will enter the world. Will it ever happen for me? Or am I barren, like so many of those women in the Old Testament?

Allison

Accepting her new kind of normal, as Allison had on Christmas Eve, did not prepare her for Sunday morning, Christmas Day, when she found herself in church with her ex-husband. It was beyond strange. How should she introduce him to her friends and neighbors? Should she identify Tony as her ex? Should she tell anyone his last name? Or should she simply try to get out of church without speaking to another soul?

She chewed on those questions throughout most of the morning service. And when it was over and the time arrived to make the first introduction, she settled for, "This is my daughter, Meredith, and her father, Tony." No one batted an eye. If anyone else thought the circumstance strange, they didn't let on.

The same had been true of Susan when she called to invite Allison and Meredith for Christmas dinner. When she'd learned Tony was also at Allison's, Susan included him in the invitation. She hadn't sounded the least surprised. And so they went to the Lyle home after church.

After the introductions were made, Meredith mentioned the nice stables out beyond the backyard and said how much she'd always liked horses. Ned offered to show her their two geldings, and they set off for the barn. Tony tagged along, leaving Allison and Susan in the kitchen.

"You've had a good Christmas," Susan said after the back door closed. It wasn't a question.

"Yes."

"I'm glad." Susan returned to cutting tomatoes for the salad.

"Can I help with something?"

"If you don't mind, you could set the table."

"I don't mind. For how many?"

"This is all of us. I invited Chet and Marsha and the boys, but Marsha said they couldn't come."

"They weren't in church this morning either." From the end of the counter, Allison picked up the wooden box holding the good silverware and carried it into the formal dining room.

In a voice loud enough for Allison to hear, Susan said, "I'm worried about Marsha. She doesn't seem able to shake her depression. She's so withdrawn."

"I guess you can't blame her." Allison moved around the table, placing the silverware on either side of the china plates. "It isn't natural for children to die before their parents. How does anyone overcome such a loss?"

"I don't know, apart from by God's help."

Allison returned to the kitchen and stopped near the window over the sink. Her gaze went to the stables and to the three people standing in its doorway. "If something ever happened to Meredith, I don't know what I'd do."

"It's every mother's nightmare. We spend so much time, especially when they are teens, praying they don't do anything too stupid."

"Growing up doesn't mean we stop making stupid mistakes." Allison turned toward her friend again.

A wry smile curved Susan's mouth. "No, it sure doesn't." She picked up the large salad bowl and carried it to the sideboard in the dining room. Then she went to the back door, opened it, and called out, "Dinner's ready. Come and get it."

Ned, Tony, and Meredith returned to the house. Tony washed

his hands in the utility room while Meredith went to the downstairs bath to do the same. Ned went upstairs to use the master bathroom. In short order, they were all gathered in the dining room. The host said grace over the meal, and then the passing of bowls and platters began.

"How much longer will you be working in Boise?" Susan asked Meredith.

"Maybe another two weeks."

"Your mom's going to miss you when you go back to Texas."

"I know. I'm going to miss her too." Meredith smiled toward Allison. "We've had a great time." She looked at Tony. "Me and Dad too."

Tony said, "Her mom and I would both like it if she could transfer back to Boise for good."

"Maybe some day, Dad, but it's not going to happen anytime soon. Not if I want to advance in the company."

And the longer you stay in Texas, the more likely it is you'll meet someone and get married, and then you'll never come home to Idaho.

Almost as if she'd heard Allison's thought, Meredith glanced toward her again. "We'll have to wait and see what comes. In today's economy, who knows what'll happen next year or the one after that. I consider myself lucky to have a job. Plenty of college grads are selling gas in convenience stores or working at Walmart because they can't find jobs in their chosen field."

"Aren't you a ray of sunshine?" Tony said in a teasing voice.

Everyone laughed, and the conversation turned in other directions, moving easily from one topic to another throughout the remainder of the meal.

Allison hated to see their time with the Lyles end. It hadn't been awkward to be there with Tony, as she'd feared it might be. And, oddly enough, when Meredith and Tony left tomorrow, she would hate to see them go. Not just Meredith. Tony too. Her feelings had changed from a week ago when she'd allowed Meredith to twist her arm about inviting him to come up for Christmas. She'd dreaded his coming, but her worry had been for nothing.

Was that because he'd been sober throughout the visit? Or was it because something had changed inside of her? Perhaps the answer was a little of both.

She felt a twinge in her heart, the familiar pain that said she'd lost what she'd most wanted. She would be wise to remember this Tony wasn't the same man who'd walked out on her and remember that the old Tony could return at any time. It was a truth she'd learned from bitter experience.

Allison

The week between Christmas and New Year's was a busy one for Allison. She used it to catch up on all of her business and personal bookkeeping. She cleaned out file drawers, both physical and electronic. She shredded private documents. Inactive but potentially important files were moved to plastic storage boxes and taken up to the attic.

Note to self: Buy a better scanner and try to go paperless in the New Year.

At the end of each day, she fell into bed, too exhausted to read or even watch television. But it was a good kind of tired.

On Friday afternoon, she drove into town to the combination video, electronics, and hardware store. The proprietress, Connie Hansen, had set aside four DVDs for Allison. It had long been a Kavanagh tradition to stay at home and ring in the new year while watching old movies. Allison looked forward to building a fire in the fireplace, filling a couple of big bowls with hot buttered popcorn, and curling up on the sofa with Meredith in front of the flat-screen TV.

"I hear tell your daughter will be headed back to Texas soon," Connie said as she placed the DVDs into a canvas sack.

Allison wished people would stop reminding her of that. "Yes. All too soon."

"Wish she could've joined us at book club while she was in Idaho. I'd've liked to meet her. Susan Lyle says she's real nice."

"You won't get any argument from me about that."

Connie leaned forward and lowered her voice, even though they were the only two people in the store. "I suppose you heard about Marsha Leonard."

"Heard what?"

"She up and left her husband and boys. Packed a bag and just took off. Don't think anyone knows where she is."

"Oh no."

Connie nodded. "Happened last Sunday, though nobody outside the family knew of it until yesterday. I hear tell Chet's beside himself with worry, not knowing where she's gone. That's the last family I'd've thought this would happen to."

Deciding Connie Hansen had moved beyond information sharing and into the realm of gossip, Allison picked up the bag that held the DVDs. "I've got to run, Connie. I need to get home before Meredith arrives from Boise."

"'Course you do. Well, you say hello to her from me, and tell her I hope to meet her next time."

"I will. Thanks." She glanced at the bag in her hands and back again. "I'll return these on Monday."

"That'll be fine. You drive careful now."

"I will."

She hurried out of the store and got into her Subaru but paused for a moment before starting the car, still digesting the news about Marsha Leonard. That must've been why none of them were in church on Sunday. Her heart went out to Chet. She understood how it felt when a spouse walked out the door, shattering the lives left behind.

Help him through this, Lord. And the boys too.

She started the engine and drove toward home, but her thoughts remained on the Leonard family. Especially on Chet. Allison wasn't a close friend of the Leonards, like the Lyles were, but they were more than mere acquaintances.

Chet seemed a good and decent man. Faithful and godly,

according to Susan. Why would Marsha leave him and her two boys? Yes, she was grieving the loss of her eldest son, but why throw away the family she had left? Marsha must've been beyond grief to think leaving those who loved her was the answer to her heartache.

Why does life have to be so hard?

The question caused her thoughts to turn from the Leonards to her great-aunt. Aunt Emma, Allison had learned from the diaries she'd read thus far, had fallen in love with a young man when she was fifteen, but he'd had eyes for Allison's grandmother, Elizabeth. The discovery surprised Allison, perhaps more than it should. Was it possible the young man in the diary was the same one who was in those photographs? He must be since he was the only—

She lost that train of thought when she saw her daughter's rental car turning into the driveway ahead of her. She hadn't expected Meredith for another hour. Must have gotten off work early.

By the time Allison pulled into the garage, Meredith was standing on the deck with her rolling suitcase.

"Hi, honey." Allison pushed the code to close the garage door. "Didn't expect you this soon." She hurried up the steps and stuck her key into the lock.

Meredith shivered. "Man, it's bitter today."

"We'll warm you up in a hurry." She held the door open for her daughter to enter first. "Coffee or hot chocolate?"

"Whichever you're fixing for yourself."

"Hot chocolate it is."

"What have you got in the bag? Our movies?"

"Uh-huh."

Meredith followed Allison into the kitchen and looked into the bag. "Oooh. You've got some good ones. Grab a new box of Kleenex. We're gonna need a bunch of tissues."

Allison laughed softly. When it came to movies, she and her daughter definitely had similar tastes. They loved to laugh and cry. The best movies made them do both.

"Can't you see Dad rolling his eyes? He never understood why we were crying through the credits and saying we loved the movie at the same time."

Yes, she could picture Tony rolling his eyes. Meredith had learned it from him.

"I hope he isn't too lonely tomorrow night," her daughter added.

Doubt raised its ugly head. "Are you worried about him?" Translation: *Are you afraid he'll fall off the wagon?*

Meredith sat on one of the kitchen stools. "No. Not really." She shrugged. "Maybe a little. But he's doing so well, Mom. I really think he'll stick with it this time."

If he can do it now, why couldn't he have stuck with it before we divorced? Allison turned toward the counter and dragged in a quick breath, ashamed of herself for slipping so easily into her old thought processes.

"Mom?"

"Hmm?"

"You're doing well too."

Allison looked over her shoulder.

"When I go back to Texas, I won't worry about you like I used to."

She smiled at her daughter. "Thanks, honey. I'm glad of that."

Emma

1928

Emma felt so light she almost believed her feet had wings.

It was the first day of autumn, and the world seemed over-laid with a buttery yellow hue. The afternoon air was warm and mellow. A few trees had begun to turn, but most of them still sported coats of green. Gardens were alive with color.

Emma walked as fast as possible, eager to get home, eager to start dinner, eager for her husband to return from work. She needed to prepare a special meal tonight. Something out of the ordinary. Something as delicious as the news she had to tell Alexander.

She was pregnant. Before next summer she would hold their baby in her arms. Alexander would like a son, of course, but Emma couldn't care less whether the baby was a boy or a girl. Healthy, that was all she cared about.

The cottage they rented was small. They would have to squeeze a crib into the single bedroom. It would be tight but manageable. Or maybe Alexander would want to move. Their finances had improved some. The doctor and hospital bills from her husband's accident last February had been paid in full. Maybe . . . just maybe . . .

But it didn't matter. If Alexander didn't want to move, then she would be happy where they were. How could she be other-wise with a baby on the way?

She turned a corner and their house came into view. Alexander's truck was in the driveway. Another automobile was parked at the curb. Her joy slipped a little, knowing her husband was home and had company. She quickened her footsteps. When she reached the house, the kitchen side door was pulled open before she could reach for the knob.

"Where've you been?" Alexander demanded, then turned his back toward her and strode into the parlor.

She followed, nerves churning.

A man—a stranger—rose from the chair in the corner. He wore a nice suit and polished shoes, but this was no gentleman. She saw that in his eyes as he looked at her. "Mrs. Monroe. We meet at last."

She glanced at her husband, waiting for an introduction. None came.

"Get our guest something to drink, Emma."

"No," the man said. "Don't bother. Time I was leaving." He set his hat on his head as he moved toward the front door. "Remember what I told you, Monroe. We don't like it when you make mistakes that cost us money."

"It won't happen again," Alexander answered.

The stranger stopped and turned to look at Emma. His slow smile caused her heart to twist in her chest. "We always collect, Monroe. One way or another. Remember that as well."

This had something to do with the bootlegging. Emma knew it as surely as if the man had announced it aloud. He was here to threaten Alexander, and to threaten her too. Her hands went to her abdomen, pressing tightly, the gesture instinctive and protective.

The door closed as the stranger left.

"What did he want?" she whispered, as if afraid he might overhear and return.

"Nothing for you to worry about." Alexander dropped onto the small sofa. "Where were you? What's for supper?"

Emma didn't want to tell him about her visit to the doctor. She didn't want to share the good news about the baby. Not now. Perhaps tomorrow, but not now.

Allison

At the stroke of midnight, Allison paused the third movie of the evening—*Steel Magnolias* was playing—and she and Meredith clinked champagne glasses filled with their favorite sodas.

"Happy New Year, Mom."

"Happy New Year, Meredith."

"I've got the feeling it's going to be a good one. Maybe the best ever, especially for you."

"I hope you're right, honey. I'd like a best-ever year."

Meredith leaned toward Allison and kissed her on the cheek. "That's what I'm going to pray for you, then. Best ever, starting in January and all the way through to December."

They both settled back into their ends of the sofa, Gizmo curled into a ball between them, and Allison pressed Play on the remote.

A best-ever year. What would that look like? Allison found it hard to imagine. Even after being alone for more than a year—two years come April—she still felt as if something or someone was missing much of the time. It helped a little, living in her new home in the mountains, and she was glad she hadn't fought Tony over their Boise house.

The funeral scene in the movie began, and Meredith immediately pressed a tissue to her eyes. Allison felt a surge of affection for her daughter and said a silent prayer of thanksgiving for the wonderful woman Meredith had become. Then she, too, reached for a tissue.

A slew of new design work came Allison's way in January, most of it the direct result of a previous client singing Allison's praises to her friends and colleagues. She was thankful for the full schedule. It helped ease the pain of Meredith's return to Texas.

With snow piled high and growing higher, poor Gizmo didn't get to go on any long walks. Mostly mistress and pooch went from the garage to the end of the plowed driveway and back again. For the sake of her own health, Allison made sure she put in forty minutes to an hour on the treadmill daily.

Despite the snowpack on the roads, Allison managed to make it into Kings Meadow for church almost every Sunday. She noticed Chet Leonard and his sons in their usual pew each week, but she didn't know what else to say to him beyond, "I'm praying for all of you."

February turned gray and grim. Not as much snow fell, but the clouds never seemed to blow away. The gloom began to press in on Allison, so she ordered a light for her desk that was supposed to treat seasonal affective disorder. It seemed to help.

When she wasn't working or exercising, Allison was trying to decide what novel to recommend to the book club in March. It was her month to choose. She read book blurbs on the Internet until her eyes crossed, and still she couldn't decide.

Days came and went, whether she paid attention to their passing or not, and while she couldn't say the start of the year felt special or best ever, she could say she was learning to be content. It was a good place to be.

Allison

Wearing a bulky cardigan, Allison stood on the front deck, smiling at the bright blue sky overhead. The thermometer on the corner of the house said it was sixty degrees and climbing. Amazing for mid-March. She didn't expect the warm weather to continue for long, and the weatherman promised it wouldn't. Cooler temps, wind, and rain—perhaps even a little more snow—would likely be the norm until May.

She didn't care. Today it felt like spring and new life and fresh hope. She felt like dancing. In fact, she thought she would.

Face toward heaven, arms outstretched, and eyes closed, she spun and hopped and dipped around the deck. Then, imagining what she must look like, she laughed.

Oh, that felt good.

Dizzy at last, she stopped and grabbed hold of the railing. Then she noticed Gizmo had moved off the deck and was sitting on the steps, watching her with eyes that said, *You've gone nuts.*

"Yes, maybe I have," she answered him—and laughed again.

She went inside, the dog zipping through the doorway ahead of her, and walked to her bedroom to change her clothes. She had a bit of shopping to do before meeting Susan for dinner, followed by the book club meeting at the library at seven.

Allison donned a pair of Levi's and a red sweatshirt with a white collar. She didn't fuss much with her hair. A ponytail would do.

With a little time to spare before she should leave, she sat at her desk and checked e-mail. She was surprised to see Tony's name pop up in the list of unread mail. She clicked on it.

> Hi, Allie. Hope you're doing well. I talked to Meredith last night. I've been thinking about flying down to see her. Maybe in May. Did you know she's met some guy? She sounds interested in him. Thinks he's special. Made me think back to when we first met in college. If she's still seeing him by the time I go down, I'll check him out. Make sure he's good enough for her. Next time you're coming to Boise, let me know. Maybe we could meet for lunch. I'd like to see you. Tony

Allison closed her e-mail and leaned back in her desk chair. Meredith had met someone special? She hadn't mentioned any guy, special or otherwise, when they'd talked on Saturday. Why would she tell her dad and not her mom? That made no sense. Meredith shared everything with Allison. Or at least that was what Allison had believed.

And what about Tony's suggestion that she meet him for lunch sometime? She wasn't sure how she felt about that. His visit over Christmas had turned out all right. But that had been for Meredith's sake. Did Allison *want* to see him apart from their daughter?

With a sigh, she stood. "Gizmo, you want to go to town?"

The dog hopped and spun in a circle.

"Yeah, I thought you would. Come on."

After ten months in their mountain home, Allison and Gizmo had their "go to town" routine down pat. They were on their way in under ten minutes, Gizmo fastened into his doggy seat belt harness. The winding highway into Kings Meadow was mostly dry now, although there were a few slick spots where sunshine never reached the road. Just in case, Allison kept her speed well below fifty.

In town, she stopped at the drug store first to pick up her thyroid prescription. Then she went to the post office to get the mail from her box followed by the dry cleaners where she dropped off a couple of sweaters. Finally, she parked her car in the lot beside the restaurant. Susan waited for her at a table near the large window overlooking the river and the mountains to the south.

"Am I late?" Allison slid onto the chair.

"No. I'm early. Ned went over to Chet's to help deliver a colt, so I didn't have to fix dinner. Left me with time on my hands." She touched the novel on the table with her right hand. It was the one the club would discuss tonight. "Gave me a chance to glance through the book and think up more questions."

"I really liked this one. I'll be reading more by the author."

"Me too. Did you decide what book we're reading for next month?"

Allison answered, "It's a young adult novel. I figured since most everyone seemed to like *The Hunger Games*, they might not mind another YA. But it's funny. I adored it. No dystopian societies in this one. Unless that's how you think of the turbulent sixties."

"Ha ha. Very funny from somebody who was still a baby at the time."

"Hey, I was four when the sixties ended."

"Like I said. A baby."

Allison felt a surge of affection for this woman who'd become such a dear friend, so important in the new life she'd built for herself.

The waiter came with glasses of water and they ordered their dinners. After he left, Susan said, "You haven't told me anything about Emma lately. Anything new from her journals?"

"Actually, yes. You know the crush she had on that young man, Alexander Monroe? The one she's written about almost from the start of her diaries? She's crazy about him, and he's still attracted to my grandmother who's about to get married."

"Well, that's understandable. His attraction to Elizabeth, I mean. Your grandmother was a rare beauty. I've always thought she looked a lot like Nicole Kidman when she was younger." Susan took a sip of water. "What year are you up to now?"

"Nineteen twenty-six. Aunt Emma was nineteen and my grandmother was eighteen."

"Are you still resisting the urge to look ahead?"

"Yes."

"You have more self-control than I do, obviously."

Allison smiled. She doubted that was true. Susan had more self-control than most anyone she knew. "Reading Aunt Emma's diaries makes me feel as if she is here with me, still telling fascinating stories about her life. I don't want to rush through them. I think I enjoy the anticipation of discovering what might happen next as much as the discovery itself."

"Don't read too slowly. There are a lot of journals to get through before that collection is ready for publication."

"You never give up, do you?"

"Not when I know something's a good idea. Think of all the collectors of Emma's photographs who would love to have a record of her life. I'm telling you, it would sell like hotcakes, and you would have a great time as the editor, choosing what to put in and what to leave out. Just think. We could have it as a book club selection."

The way she said it, Susan did make it sound fun. But Allison had to wonder, would Aunt Emma approve?

Emma

John was in Seattle on business when Liza's water broke and labor began, a full three weeks ahead of her due date. By providence, Emma and Alexander were visiting when it happened.

"Call for the doctor, Alexander," Emma said as she helped her sister to her feet. "I'll see to Liza until he gets here."

"And please . . ." Liza touched her belly, grimacing. "Please let my mother know the baby is coming. I want her with me if possible."

"I'll make the call," he answered as he reached out to touch the back of Liza's hand, "and then I'll go get your mother and bring her back myself. Don't worry, Elizabeth. I'll see to it." There was a tenderness in Alexander's voice that Emma never heard when he spoke to her.

He wishes she were his wife. He wishes the baby about to be born were his.

The knowledge struck Emma like a blow to the stomach. Nothing had changed in all of these months. Even married to Emma and her carrying his child, Alexander's thoughts were for another woman. His thoughts were for her sister. The tragic thing was, it didn't alter how Emma felt about him. Not a bit. She would do anything for him. She would turn herself inside out. She would even die for him. Why couldn't he see that?

Is that how he feels about Liza?

"Emma?" Her sister's voice cracked. "Help me upstairs to the bedroom, please."

Yanked from her thoughts, Emma answered, "Yes. Right away. Come on."

They moved out of the parlor and up the stairs, pausing when Liza felt another hard pain. "It's happening so much faster than last time," Liza said when she could draw breath again. "I don't believe this baby is going to wait for Dr. Thompson to get here."

Emma found that a terrifying notion. She knew next to nothing about childbirth. "Of course he'll get here in time." She tightened her arm around Liza's back. "Let's get you into bed so you can relax."

"Thank you, Emma. You . . . you're the best sister in the world."

"Hardly that."

They continued up the stairs.

In the bedroom Emma helped Liza out of her dress, into a nightgown, and onto the bed. She tried not to show her alarm at the ever-increasing frequency and intensity of Liza's contractions. Wasn't labor supposed to build slowly? She prayed the doctor would hurry.

At one point Liza took hold of Emma's hand. "I'm glad our babies will be close to the same age. They'll be like siblings. They'll love each other. Like you and me."

Emma nodded.

The Hendricks' cook—a short, plump woman with a cap of gray curls and a round, ruddy face—appeared in the bedroom doorway. "Mary told me the mistress was having her baby. I come to see for myself." Her London origins revealed themselves in her accent.

"Mrs. Willows." Emma hurried toward the woman. "I don't know what to do until the doctor arrives. The contractions are very close together."

"Well then, you'll be comforted to know I've delivered several babies without help from any old sawbones." She began rolling up her sleeves. "Bring blankets, clean towels, and a pair of scissors. Twine too. And have Mary boil water." She stopped and gave Emma a sharp look. "And if you plan to faint, I'll have you leave the room now and not come back. There'll be no time for tending to you with a baby on the way."

"I'm not going to faint."

"Good. I thought you were made of sterner stuff, Mrs. Monroe. You remind me of myself when I was young and thin." She barked a laugh. "Though nobody believes I was ever either of those, I'm sure."

Emma didn't feel strong, but she hoped the woman was right about her being made of sterner stuff.

Allison

Tony met Allison inside the Boise restaurant. It was a Monday, half an hour before the lunchtime rush, and they were able to be seated at once.

After the hostess left, Tony drew a small gift-wrapped box from his pocket and slid it across the table. "Happy birthday a day late."

"Tony, you shouldn't—"

"Sure I should." He motioned with his head. "Go on. Open it."

Feeling off-kilter, she plucked the tape loose and removed the wrapping paper. A black velvet jewelry box was inside. She lifted her eyes to meet his gaze.

How many of her birthdays had Tony forgotten over the years? Far more than he'd remembered. And even when he remembered, how often had she received a gift? Or even a card? Christmases too. Familiar resentment coiled in her stomach. Old hurts rushed back. Almost a year divorced, and still she wasn't free of them.

"Go on," he repeated softly. "Open it."

Holding her breath, she raised the hinged lid on the box. Inside lay a pair of opal earrings.

"You always liked opals."

It surprised her he knew that.

"Meredith told me they're one of your favorites."

Meredith. Of course. Tony wouldn't have remembered yesterday was her birthday if their daughter hadn't reminded him.

He certainly wouldn't have known Allison's fondness for this particular gemstone without Meredith's help.

"I missed a lot of your birthdays," he added. "I was there, but I wasn't. I'm sorry, Allie. Truly sorry."

"It's water under the bridge. It doesn't matter anymore."

"Sure it matters. It matters to me even if it doesn't matter to you."

That was the thing. It *did* matter to her, and she didn't want it to.

He must have sensed her discomfort, for he changed the subject. "I got my six-month sobriety chip the other night."

Allison's jaw clenched. Why on earth had she agreed to meet Tony for lunch? Why had she ever bothered to reply to the e-mail he'd sent a couple of weeks ago. Being with him brought up too much garbage, too many bad memories. Their time together at Christmas, as pleasant as it was, hadn't erased the past. It couldn't.

"I wish I'd caught on to working the steps for my addictions as quickly as you did for codependency."

She shrugged, not knowing what to say to that. Judging by her reactions over the last few minutes, she wasn't sure she'd caught on to anything. Maybe she hadn't made a shred of progress in recovering from her own hurts, hang-ups, and habits. Maybe all she'd done was pretend for months and months. When Tony was out of her sight, he was out of her mind. When he was out of her mind, she became sane—but not necessarily healthy.

Tony said, "I made a mess of things. That's no secret."

"Yes, you did."

"If I had it to do over again—"

"Stop, Tony. That kind of thinking is useless. We don't get to change the past. All we can hope is to do things differently in the future."

A waitress came and took their order. Allison didn't think

she would be able to eat when the food came. Her stomach felt like stone.

"Allie?"

She looked at Tony again.

"I didn't get to say this when I was with you at Christmas. Let me say it now. Please."

"Fine. If you need to, go ahead."

"When I walked out that day, after you told me to get sober or leave, I left in anger. I didn't mean to stay away. Not more than a night or two. I sure didn't think you would stick to your guns to not *let* me return until I sobered up for good. Even then, I believed I could control my drinking anytime I wanted without any help from anyone. Without any help from God. A God who remained a stranger to me." He raked the fingers of one hand through his hair. "I was a fool."

A lump formed in Allison's throat.

"I loved you, Allie. I did. Still do, though I know you don't want to hear it. Probably can't believe me. But I can see now how selfish I was. Even my love for you and Meredith was about me and my needs and wants and not about either of you. In many ways, as a husband, I left you emotionally, even physically, long before I walked out on you. As a dad . . ." He let his words fade into silence.

How many years had Allison wished and hoped and prayed for Tony to say something like that to her? So many. Too many.

"Recovery is something I have to do one day at a time and with God's help."

"I know," she whispered. "All of life has to be lived that way."

He looked as if he was about to say more, then shook his head.

Allison wanted to leave. She was getting a headache, felt the throb strengthening in her temples. Her nerves jangled. But their lunch arrived right then. She hoped something to eat would help her feel better.

"Mind if I say a blessing?" Tony asked.

"No. Go ahead."

For the remainder of the meal, they talked only of Meredith—the safest of topics—and Allison made her escape as soon after as possible.

———

An ache in her heart replaced all other feelings as Allison drove up the state highway toward home. An ache . . . and anger too. Tony had tried to manipulate her at lunch. He *had* manipulated her, and she shouldn't have let him do it. She'd allowed it too often in the past.

"Mind if I say a blessing?"

She *had* minded. It was an act. Tony's Christianity had always been a surface thing. Was he even saved? Could someone be a Christian and a drunk at the same time?

Allison winced at the thought. God had called her to task on that kind of thinking a number of years ago, and the memory of it was seared into her brain. As she'd read the first few verses of Romans 14, she'd felt God say, *Who are you, Allison, to pass judgment on another? Tony belongs to Me, and I am able to make him stand.*

"So why *didn't* You make him stand?" she whispered.

Seeing a pull-off ahead, she flipped her right turn signal and slowed her vehicle. Once she stopped the Subaru, she turned off the engine and leaned her forehead against the steering wheel.

I'm still demanding to know why. I don't mean to do it, Father. I don't want to do it. I thought I was learning to be content, and now here I am again. In the same place.

"How pathetic," she added aloud.

Lifting her head, she looked out the windshield. A thin blanket of snow covered the mountainsides, but the pine trees had shed their white winter cloaks. Everything was beautiful and still, the only sounds rising from the river on the opposite side of the highway.

Help me, Lord. I'm tired of sliding backward into old resentments. Help me move forward and forgive. Really forgive.

Allison

The public library in Kings Meadow was surprisingly good for such a small community. Allison enjoyed spending time there. Sometimes she liked to simply stroll the aisles, dragging an index finger along a row of books, reading the titles as she went, pulling one out when it caught her eye. Sometimes serendipity brought a greater reward.

But on this weekday morning in April, the week after her birthday, she was depending upon the Dewey Decimal System as she sought information about tracing one's ancestry as well as books about the history of Idaho in the early twentieth century. She was frowning, concentrating hard on titles, when a man spoke her name.

"Morning, Allison."

She turned and found Chet Leonard standing nearby. "Good morning." She smiled. "I thought I was the only non-librarian in the place at this hour."

"Me too."

"How are the boys?"

"Pretty good." He paused a moment, then added, "Their mother called earlier in the week, and they got to talk to her briefly."

Allison tried not to show her surprise. There hadn't been a word about Marsha's whereabouts since she left. Or so Susan had told her a couple of weeks ago.

Chet answered the questions Allison was too polite to ask.

"Marsha's in Nevada. Been there this whole time. She's filed for divorce. Doesn't want to come back home. Not ever. Doesn't even want joint custody of the boys."

"Oh, Chet. I'm sorry."

"Marsha was always a devoted mother. She loved our sons with everything in her. This isn't like her. This isn't like the woman I've known all these years. I wanted to go down to Reno so we could talk face-to-face, but she refused to let me come. Refused to give me her address." He closed his eyes for a few moments. "I don't know how to help her. I only know she *needs* help."

"I'm sorry," Allison repeated, softer this time.

"We had a good marriage. We had a happy family. I thought our faith could carry us through anything. Even Rick's death. Now I don't know what to think."

It might have seemed strange to someone else, the way Chet opened up to her just now. Their friendship was of a more casual nature. But Allison understood the reasons for it. There had been times in the past, as her world crashed around her ears, when she'd revealed intimate details to complete strangers. Words had poured out unexpectedly, as if she'd had no control over them. All she'd needed was a warm body who seemed willing to listen. That was what she was for Chet Leonard at the moment. A warm body willing to listen.

She offered him an understanding smile. "I wish I had words of wisdom to share with you, Chet. I was devastated when my marriage failed. But it does get easier with time. I promise you that."

His return smile was halfhearted at best.

"If there's anything I can do, Chet, just ask."

He shook his head, then shrugged. "Thanks. I appreciate the offer. I really do." He took a step back. "I'd best be on my way. Got work to get done at the ranch."

Allison watched him disappear around the end of the ceiling-high bookshelf.

A hard knot formed in the pit of her stomach. The enjoyment of browsing books in the library was gone. She felt as if she might cry. Perhaps an overreaction to the news about Marsha, but emotions weren't always logical. She'd learned that during her separation from Tony. How many times had she walked down the grocery aisle and been overcome with tears when she wasn't even thinking about him or their situation? Or how many times had she driven along a familiar road and started crying because of a song on the radio? Her emotions had been all over the map. Rarely had they been trustworthy.

She took the books she'd selected earlier to the counter and checked them out, then went outside into the morning sunshine. After letting Gizmo out of the car for a short bit of business, she drove toward home. Warm temperatures had been melting the snowpack faster than she'd anticipated. Some places were bare where a few weeks ago snow had been piled high. Spring was definitely in the air. Next time she was in Boise, she would go to the garden supply store. Some large planters filled with flowers would be welcome additions to her large deck. It faced south and got enough sun.

Maybe she should buy some new deck furniture. It would be fun to entertain more during the summer months. She could invite the book club to meet at her house in August when the days were long and the evenings pleasant.

When she got home, she dropped her purse and keys onto the table inside the front door. The light was blinking on her phone, telling her she had voice mail waiting. She picked up the handset and tapped in her code. The message was from her mom with the wonderful news that she and Allison's dad were driving to Idaho for a visit.

Excited, Allison didn't finish listening to the message. She hung up and pressed the preprogrammed button to dial her parents. Her mom answered on the third ring.

"Mom, when are you coming?"

"Didn't I tell you in the message? I thought I did. We're coming next month. For a couple of weeks."

"Oh, Mom. That's great. You'll stay with me, of course. I can hardly wait to see you. It's been too long."

"You could've come down to see us anytime, you know."

"I know. But with moving and with my work—"

"Excuses. Excuses."

Her mom was right. Those reasons *were* excuses. But Allison had needed this past year to get her legs under her, to begin to feel a little more whole. She'd made progress, although her recent lunch with Tony had shown she hadn't progressed enough.

"After we see you, we'll go to Seattle for a month to visit Chuck and Joan and to attend Karen's graduation."

Karen's graduation! Allison flinched. She'd received an invitation to her niece's high school graduation a couple of months ago but had set it aside and then forgotten about it.

"You should come with us, Allison. Chuck and Joan have plenty of room in their house, and we could take you back home on our return to Arizona."

"I couldn't be away from my work for that long. Not for a whole month. And what about Gizmo? Boarding him would be ridiculously expensive, and I wouldn't want him spending that much time in a kennel anyway."

"I'd forgotten about your dog. Pets can be so inconvenient at times."

"Maybe I could drive with you to Seattle and then fly back after Karen's graduation. That would work."

"It's settled, then. That's what we'll plan on. I'll tell your father. He'll be delighted."

Emma

1928

Liza was safely delivered of a baby boy, aided by Mrs. Willows. Mark Thomas, the name chosen for a son, weighed in at five and a half pounds—they would later learn—and had a good set of lungs. The doctor arrived about ten minutes after the baby made his entrance into the world. There was little left for the physician to do other than verify that Liza and Mark Thomas were both in fine health. Emma's and Liza's mother and Alexander got to the house soon after.

Emma stood with her back against the wall, watching the exchange of smiles and hugs, hearing the laughter and words of delight. The room was warm with joy.

Will it ever be like this for me?

She closed her eyes, fearing she might start to cry. Hurt feelings left a metallic taste on her tongue.

"Emma?"

The voice broke through her thoughts and she opened her eyes.

Her mother stood before her. "Are you all right, dear?"

Emma nodded.

"Are you sure? You look pale. Elizabeth says you helped deliver the baby."

"I didn't do all that much. I just did whatever Mrs. Willows told me to do. She knew exactly what to do." She offered a weak smile.

"I hope it hasn't made you afraid of your own delivery."

"Not at all. I've never witnessed anything more amazing in my life."

Her mother shook her head. "I'm glad of that, dear." She dropped her voice to a whisper. "But it would be better not to speak of such things in mixed company."

Emma glanced toward the bed. Liza was cradling the baby near her breast, already looking refreshed. As if she hadn't gone through hard labor a short while before. Alexander stood by a window, looking out at the backyard. None of them cared what she'd said to her mother. Even if they had, it wasn't as if they weren't all married adults, fully aware of the facts of conception and at least partially aware of the facts of giving birth. Her mother's admonition seemed a ridiculous one.

But Pearl Carter had been born into a different world. She clung to the traditions of the nineteenth century. She thought telephones were noisy, disruptive things. She thought motorcars smelly and unsightly. She was disinterested in moving pictures and had never joined the rest of the country in its excitement over radio. And she certainly believed no woman should discuss intimate subjects such as childbirth in front of a man. Not even in front of her own husband.

Her mother turned away from Emma. "Alexander, your wife is tired. I think you need to take her home now. She needs to rest."

Alexander turned from the window, nodded, and headed for the bedroom door without a word to anyone. Emma knew he expected her to follow. She pasted on a smile and pretended not to notice his rude departure as she walked to the bed and kissed her sister's cheek.

"I love you, Liza. I'm so happy for you. How blessed you are."

"Thank you, Em. I am blessed." She smiled in return.

"When will John be home?"

"In the morning."

"He'll be sorry to have missed this." She squeezed Liza's hand. "I'll come again soon after you've gotten some rest."

Liza smiled and nodded.

Emma bid her mother good-bye, then hurried out of the bedroom and down the stairs. Alexander waited for her by the truck. He wore a frown, and when she saw it she knew his mercurial mood had turned foul.

As soon as they were pulling away from the curb, he said, "I get so tired of having my nose rubbed in John Hendricks's success."

"What do you mean? Who did that?"

He ignored her questions. "And since when does your mother think she can boss me around like that?"

"She didn't—"

"Alexander," he said in a high-pitched voice, "your wife is tired. Take her home."

Emma wanted to argue with him, but she pressed her lips together to keep from it.

"I'm sick of it, Emma. Sick of them."

Sick of me too?

They drove the remainder of the way home in silence.

Allison

Allison sat at the dining room table, completed scrapbooks and loose photographs scattered across the polished surface. She held one black-and-white photo in her hand. A photograph of Aunt Emma's husband, Alexander James Monroe. Emma's *husband*. Her aunt had been married. How was that possible? Allison's mother hadn't known about it. Neither Aunt Emma nor Grandmother Elizabeth had ever said a word to anyone in the family. Aunt Emma had used her maiden name all the years Allison had known her. She'd been buried under her maiden name. But at one time, there had been a husband. At one time, she'd been Emma Monroe.

Which explained the old wedding dress Allison had discovered. The dress hadn't belonged to another woman. It had been *Emma's*. She'd worn it on her *own* wedding day. A day long kept a secret. A wedding and yet among all the many, many photographs her aunt had kept in her trunks, there wasn't a single one to commemorate her wedding day. She'd kept other photos of Alexander James Monroe. Why not any of their wedding?

Allison studied the photograph in her hand. As she'd thought before, Alexander Monroe reminded her of a silent film star. Swept-back hair that appeared to be dark blond. His eyes must have been a piercing blue. At least that was how they appeared in this snapshot. There was something brooding about his looks. And if the diaries could be believed, he'd married Emma while loving her sister. While loving Allison's grandmother!

Poor Aunt Emma.

Every family had secrets of one kind or another, but some secrets were buried deeper than others. How many years had Allison managed to keep Tony's drinking a secret from her parents, from her friends, from the pastor and elders of their church? Much longer than she should have been able or should have tried.

She picked up another photograph, this one of her aunt as a young woman. Emma Carter hadn't been a stunning beauty like her sister, Elizabeth, but she'd been pretty in her own way. Allison had always assumed she hadn't married out of choice. Because she'd been a woman of strong opinions and unafraid to face the world alone and on her own terms. That was the Emma Carter she'd known.

But it wasn't the Emma of these latest diaries. The ones from the later 1920s. Oh, there were glimpses of her here and there, but there was also someone who always seemed to come in second to her younger, prettier sister. A young woman who wasn't certain who she was or if she was good enough to deserve more than what she had. A young woman who had tried to change herself in order to please the man she loved.

"Why did you marry him, Aunt Emma, knowing what you did? Was he worth it?"

For the first time, she was tempted to pull out more diaries and skim through them until she found answers to her questions. But she refused to give in to that particular temptation. She was convinced Aunt Emma would want her to read them in order. Perhaps it was a silly conviction, but she would heed it.

Allison leaned back in her chair and thought about Tony. She'd known when they were dating that he liked to have a drink. But she'd never seen him drink to excess, never seen the slightest hint that he might have a problem. Maybe it should have bothered her more, as a Christian, but she'd never thought abstinence from alcohol was a law for believers. Everything in moderation. She'd believed that was a good rule for life. Everything in moderation.

Should she have seen beyond the facade, understood more of what she did see? Or maybe she had understood and refused to admit it. Maybe, like her great-aunt, she'd married despite what she knew or suspected.

She picked up a different photograph of Alexander. "Who are you, Mr. Monroe? And what happened that caused Aunt Emma and Grandmother to keep her marriage to you a secret all those years?"

Emma

October 2, 1928

I miscarried in the night. Yesterday Liza gave birth to a healthy baby boy, and I was present to see his entry into the world. But before the sun rose this morning, my baby was taken from me, lost in a flow of blood.

Why did this happen? Have I sinned in some horrible way? Is God punishing me? Is something wrong with me? Don't I deserve any happiness?

Alexander said it was all right. That there would be other babies. But I felt him move further away from me, even as he said it.

I wish I had died in the night too. This pain is too great to bear. Mother would say I was doomed for wishing such a thing, but I cannot help it. It's how I feel. And doesn't God already know how I feel? It can't be a surprise to Him if I admit those feelings here in this diary or even say them aloud.

October 22, 1928

The sadness never leaves me. Mother tells me I must stop mourning, fix myself up, make myself attractive for my husband, learn to smile again. She does not know how alone I am in my grief. Even Liza, who has lost a child, does not understand. Because she had John to hold her and love her and cherish her. I have no one. Least of all Alexander.

That man came to the house again yesterday. The one Alexander works for nights, making his deliveries. I was alone when he came. He said almost nothing. He did nothing that should have made me afraid, but I was afraid all the same. There is a strangeness about him, an air of danger in the way he moves, in his eyes. He said his name is Smith. Hal Smith.

Alexander is afraid of him too. I could see that when I mentioned Mr. Smith's visit. Then he left without eating his supper. Later, I cried myself to sleep. I do not know when he came home.

What has happened to my life? I feel it unraveling and cannot seem to stop it. God, help me.

Allison

In the myriad of conversations taking place before the start of book club, Allison overheard the Leonards' names mentioned numerous times. The news of Chet and Marsha's impending divorce had become general knowledge, and Allison felt sorry for Chet and his boys. It was never fun to be the object of gossip. Especially for the ones left behind.

Allison was thankful when Susan called the meeting to order. The members sat on chairs placed in a wide circle. A few matters of business were discussed, and then the meeting was turned over to Allison.

She felt a little nervous as she opened with a few of her own thoughts about the book she'd chosen for them to read. What if no one had liked her selection? And even if they had liked it, what if they had nothing to say about it tonight? Trivial worries. When, since she'd joined the book club last year, had these women failed to freely voice their opinions about a book? Not even once.

The next hour passed in a blur of animated discussion, and before she knew it, the meeting was over and members began to disperse.

"That went well," Susan said.

Allison smiled, satisfaction warming her insides. Tonight's meeting had made her feel as if she'd taken one step more into this tight-knit mountain community. She'd come to Kings Meadow because circumstances demanded it. It had seemed her only option. It no longer felt that way. She would choose to live here, no matter where else she could go.

Was that how it had been for Aunt Emma? Had she come to the mountains to hide and lick her wounds? What Allison wouldn't give to be able to sit down with her great-aunt and ask the questions she hadn't known to ask before her aunt passed away.

Drawing a deep breath, Allison slipped the strap of her purse over her shoulder. "I keep feeling like God wants to teach me something through Aunt Emma's life. Do you think that's silly?"

"No. I don't think it's silly. If God can speak through a donkey like He did in the Old Testament, then He can just as easily talk through words written in the past."

"Aunt Emma's circumstances weren't the same as mine. Not that I can see thus far."

"I don't believe they have to be the same. I had the Lord reveal a truth to me when I was looking at a wildflower growing through a crack in a rock."

Allison leaned over and gave Susan a tight hug. "Do you know how thankful I am for our friendship?"

"Likewise."

They turned in unison and headed for the glass doors of the library. Darkness had fallen over the town while they were in their meeting, but it was relieved somewhat by a half-moon floating above the eastern range. Their cars were parked side by side under a light in the parking lot. They walked over to them and stopped in front of Allison's SUV.

"Thanks for inviting me to be part of the book club. I've enjoyed it so much."

"Well, your book choice was a great one. Lots of good thoughts. I'm just sorry for the talk that went on before we got started."

"You mean about Chet and Marsha."

Susan nodded.

"Yes, I was sorry to hear it too. I saw Chet here at the library last week and he told me about the divorce. How's he holding up?"

"Okay some days. Not so good on others."

"I know how that is."

"Ned tries to be there for him as much as possible. Of course, Chet's one of those independent cowboy types. Strong. Kind of quiet and thoughtful. You know what I mean."

It was Allison's turn to nod.

"In some ways I think this is harder for Chet than not knowing where Marsha was. At least then he could believe his wife would return to him. He doesn't have much hope for that now."

"They seemed a happy couple."

Her expression sad, Susan drew a deep breath and released it slowly. "I guess this is a good reminder that things aren't always what they seem."

"No, they aren't."

"All I know to do is to pray for them."

"God hates divorce. He doesn't hate the divorced." Allison gave a slight shrug of her shoulders. "That's what Mom said to me when I was hurting and in such despair."

A small smile bowed Susan's mouth. "I'm glad you aren't in despair any longer."

"Me too."

They bid each other good night and got into their respective vehicles.

On the drive home, Allison's thoughts turned again to Chet and Marsha, and she prayed both of them would find peace. "Your will be done, Father," she whispered when she didn't know what more to pray, then added, "In my life too, Lord. Your will be done in my life too."

Allison

Allison was as excited as a kid on Christmas as she awaited the arrival of her parents on that first Saturday in May. She found herself returning to the deck again and again, hoping to catch a glimpse of their car as they turned into her driveway. It was just before four in the afternoon when she finally got her wish.

As the car approached the house, she waved her arm in a big arc, grinning like a fool. She told Gizmo to sit and stay. Then she hurried down the steps so she could hug her parents the instant she could get to them.

Her mother was out before the engine died. Tall and slender like her mother had been before her, Maggie Knight looked a couple of decades younger than her seventy-two years, despite having let her hair go gray. Whenever someone mentioned her more youthful appearance, she was quick to declare she could take no credit for it. "Good genes," she would always say. "I inherited good genes."

"Look at you, Mom. You've got a bit of a tan."

"We've been golfing a lot," her mom answered.

Allison hurried to the opposite side of the car as her dad disembarked.

A couple of years older than his wife, Robert Knight looked closer to his real age, but he also was in great physical shape. All that golfing, no doubt. He still had a full head of hair, hair that used to be as black as ink and was now a rich silver-gray. The kind of silver that women paid a hundred dollars or more to achieve in a beauty salon.

"Dad, you look fit as a fiddle."

"Feel fit, thanks. And you don't look so bad yourself, Allison. We've missed you, honey." He embraced her.

"I've missed you both too. Come inside. I'll get your bags in a bit. Are you hungry? We can eat sooner rather than later if you want."

"We're fine," he answered. "We can wait. Can't we, Maggie? I need a bit of exercise more than food. Mind if I walk about outside before I come in?"

"I don't mind, Dad. Go ahead." Allison returned to her mom's side, and the two women walked to the stairs and went up the steps to the deck. "Mom, meet Gizmo."

Maggie Knight bent down and stroked the dog's head. "Hello, boy." As she straightened, she added, "He's well-behaved."

"Not always, but for the most part."

When they entered the house, her mom stopped again. "My goodness. I didn't expect the place to look so different."

"I've added my own touches."

"You've done more than that, sweetheart. Even with all the modernizations, it always felt like a cabin when Aunt Emma was living. You've made it feel more homey."

The praise felt good. "Thanks. I've tried."

Her mom moved toward the framed photographs on the wall. "Are these some of the photos you found in the trunks?" She perused more of them on the mantel and a side table.

"Yes. And those I haven't framed, I've put in scrapbooks. I finished the last of them earlier this week. Well, except for duplicates or similar shots. I left those in a box."

"Did you frame one of that mystery man you asked about?"

"No. But I have a surprise for you about him." She hesitated a moment for effect before saying, "He was Aunt Emma's husband."

The look on her mom's face as she turned around was priceless. "Husband? Aunt Emma was never married."

"Yes, she was. She wrote about her wedding and her honeymoon in her diary."

"I don't believe it."

"Well, it's true, whether you believe it or not. And what's more, she wrote that Alexander Monroe was in love with Grandma Elizabeth when he married Aunt Emma."

Maggie stiffened. "I don't believe that either. My mother never had eyes for anyone but my father."

"I didn't say Grandma returned his feelings. It's actually quite sad to read about."

"If there were any truth to it, we would have been told years ago. Who could keep that kind of secret for so many years? Especially these days with the Internet and such."

"The secret-keeping began long before computers and the web. Maybe even before you were born. It would have been easier back in the thirties and forties to hide information. Would you like to see some of the diary entries about him?"

Her mother shook her head. "Maybe later. It really isn't important, after all. Everyone it might have mattered to is dead."

Allison could have argued. It mattered to her. For some reason, it mattered a lot. But she sensed her mom wouldn't understand, even if she tried to explain it. And she probably couldn't explain it. Not yet. Not until she read more of the journals.

Her dad knocked on the glass door from the back deck off the kitchen. Gizmo barked as he raced to see who it was. Allison followed at a more sedate pace.

"It's drying up nicely," he said when the door slid open. "I remember the snow still being neck deep on the first of May some years."

"I remember that too. I thought it would be that way this year. The snow was really deep all winter long. But the warmer temps have melted it fast."

Her dad grinned. "You look good, kid. Awful good. Lighter. Like a burden's been lifted. It's good to see you like this."

Glad you didn't see me a year ago when I was a mess.

Her dad insisted on going with Allison to bring in their luggage. Then she left her folks in the guest bedroom to settle in while she went downstairs to see to the remainder of the supper preparations.

It surprised her, how completely natural it felt to have her parents here. In so many ways it was as if this had been her home for years and years. She looked forward to taking her mom and dad to church in the morning. She wanted them to meet her friends and many acquaintances. She wanted them to know she was in a better place. Emotionally as well as physically. Spiritually too, although God was still remodeling her heart. A major project, to be sure.

Emma

1929

Emma stared at her reflection in the mirror. When had she become the woman who looked back at her? Not only the sad turn of her mouth or the dark circles beneath her eyes. When had she become a woman without an opinion, someone who seemed afraid of her own shadow, someone who entertained self-pity in the night? What happened to the little girl who loved to climb trees and ride horses bareback and swing from a rope on the tree and drop into a pond? Liza had asked her a similar question once, but Emma hadn't been willing or able to see that she was right.

"Where did you go?" Emma whispered. "Are you still in there somewhere?"

She leaned closer to the mirror.

What sort of person lets herself disappear in order to please another? Like a chameleon, always changing colors.

Whom have I pleased? Not Alexander.

Not God either.

She'd drifted away from the Lord. Not on purpose. Through neglect. She rarely picked up her Bible. She seldom prayed. She hadn't gone to church in a long, long time. Alexander refused to go, and it had become easier to simply stay home with him than to make him angry when she went alone.

Easier. Was that how she made her choices today? She would do this because it was easier. She would do that because it was easier.

"Easier is not necessarily better," she told her reflection.

Somehow, Emma had to find her way back to her true self. She hadn't lost herself in a day. She wouldn't find her way back in a day. But she could take the first step. She could start looking.

She turned from the mirror and picked up her Bible from the nightstand, wiping away the fine layer of dust on its cover with her free hand. Then she retrieved her bound journal from its hiding place and carried both books to the table in the kitchen.

"Lord, help me." She let the Bible fall open and began to read.

Allison

Pastor Josh preached a sermon on courage that Sunday morning, and Allison felt as if he'd prepared it for her alone. That wasn't an unusual experience. It was often that way these days.

It seemed most of the congregation waited outside to meet her parents when the service was over. She was on a first-name basis with everyone, and it was fun to make the introductions. Time and again she heard someone tell her parents how glad they were to have Allison living in the Kings Meadow area. Two women said what a terrific addition she was to the book club. And Chet Leonard said he was grateful for the encouragement she'd been to him in recent months, although he didn't go into specifics.

"My, what a handsome man," her mom said as they walked toward Allison's car later. "Is he single?"

"Mom, don't start matchmaking."

"Well, *is* he single?"

"He's about to be divorced. Maybe he is by now."

Her mother cocked an eyebrow. "I think he likes you."

"Don't be ridiculous." Allison pressed the button on the key fob to unlock the doors of the SUV. "He's still in love with his wife."

"Hmm."

Susan Lyle had invited Allison and her parents to Sunday dinner, so she turned the car east when pulling out of the parking lot and drove toward her friend's house.

From the backseat, her mom recalled meeting Susan years before. "She was very close friends with your aunt. Does she know anything about that mystery man you believe was Emma's husband?"

"No. Not a thing. And if Aunt Emma would have told anyone, I think she would have told Susan."

"Exactly. So it must not be true. But I don't want to talk about him. I want to know more about that cowboy. Leonard. Was that his name?"

Allison released an exaggerated sigh.

Her mom laughed.

"You're hopeless, Mom. You know that?"

"I know, but you love me anyway."

"Yes, I do." Allison glanced at her dad, seated to her right. "You too, Dad."

"Thanks, my girl."

Her mom's voice turned serious. "I can't help wanting you to be with someone, Allison. I hate the thought of you being lonely."

"I know that too. But I think it's good for me to be alone right now. I'm in a good place. Really and truly I am. Maybe I needed to learn to be alone with myself so I can learn to be better with another if the time comes."

"My goodness," her mom replied. "That sounded wise."

"Didn't it, though."

As all three of them laughed, Allison sent up a silent thanks to God for the parents He'd given her. She knew men and women who hadn't spoken to their fathers or mothers or both for years because of some rift or another. She didn't believe that could happen with her parents. Oh, she could disagree with them at times. Strongly disagree. But love ruled, even in an argument. How grateful she was for that example.

Allison pulled up to the Lyles' house with those words of thanksgiving in her mind.

By the time Allison had turned off the engine, Susan stood in her doorway, smiling and waving. "Welcome," she said as Allison and her parents walked toward her. "Maggie. Bob. I'm so glad you could come. The last time I saw you was at Emma's funeral, but we didn't get a chance to talk."

"I'm not surprised," Maggie answered. "There were a lot of people at the funeral."

"She was dearly loved by everyone in Kings Meadow. She was an institution, really." Susan motioned for her guests to go inside, then she brought up the rear. "Would any of you like something to drink? It will be about half an hour before dinner is ready."

Susan Lyle was the kind of hostess who made everyone feel important and special. Allison sensed it wasn't something Susan had learned to do over time. It was innate. One of the gifts of the Spirit—the gift of hospitality.

Conversation around the dinner table eventually turned back to Aunt Emma. Susan shared a number of stories that were new to Allison and her mother. "Did you know she took flying lessons when she was older than I am now?"

"Flying lessons?" Maggie Knight shook her head. "When was this?"

Susan frowned in thought. "Maybe nineteen seventy-two or -three. Ned and I hadn't been married more than five years." She looked toward her husband for confirmation. "Am I right?"

He laughed. "I haven't a clue. All the years tend to run together. But I do remember her talking about those lessons. She was right proud of herself."

Allison thought about the Emma Carter she was discovering in the pages of the diaries. That younger Emma didn't seem particularly adventurous or courageous. And yet, those traits had been very much true of the aunt Allison knew as a child. Growing old hadn't slowed Aunt Emma down much either. Not until almost the end of her life.

"And do *you* think my aunt was married when she was younger?" Her mother's question pulled Allison's attention to the present.

Susan gave a small smile. "I must believe it, Maggie. Emma had no reason to lie in her diaries. Not any reason I can think of, at any rate."

"Why keep it a secret?" Allison's mother pressed. "Why use her maiden name the rest of her life?"

"I don't know that either." Susan looked at Allison. "But I do believe Emma meant for Allison to find her diaries and read them. And eventually Allison will discover the answers to your questions and her own questions too."

Emma

The crash of 1929 was felt immediately by people like John Hendricks and his parents. People with money. People with investments in the stock market. People who owned businesses. It embarrassed Emma to see the smug satisfaction in her husband's eyes when he learned the Hendricks family had lost so much.

"They won't be sticking their noses in the air anymore," he crowed. "How the mighty have fallen!"

She could have told him that for all her sister's husband and in-laws had lost in the stock market, they were far from destitute. They hadn't lost their homes and cars. They could still afford their servants. She could have warned him not to be so pleased about the troubles of others because the Monroes just might have to turn to the Hendrickses for help one day.

She could have but she didn't.

Alexander ceased to gloat when the effects of the crash began to trickle down to people like him. And trickle down they did. First Alexander's hours at the mill were reduced. Then he was let go. Even his bootlegging business fell off; his customers didn't have money to buy the bathtub gin. By late summer the Monroes were evicted from the cottage they'd rented since the summer they married, and with no other options, they moved into her parents' home.

October 2, 1930

Alexander leaves the house every morning to look for work. Or so he tells me. Most days he doesnt return until long after dark. When he does, he is still unemployed. He smells of liquor when he comes in. Sometimes he is so drunk I'm surprised he can make it up the stairs to our bedroom. Last night, when he crawled into bed beside me, there was a new smell. Perfume. Cheap perfume. There is only one way I know of for him to smell like that. He was with some other woman. A woman who was close enough to him for her perfume to get on his clothes and skin.

I am sick at heart. Sometimes I think I cannot draw another breath for the pain of it. I've known he cared more for Liza than for me. But since she would never betray me or John, I wasnt afraid Alexander would do anything more than long for her from afar. I still had hope he could learn to love me. But now?

I have tried to be a good wife. I have tried to obey him as I promised in my wedding vows. I have tried not to nag, like the steady drip of water Proverbs talks about. But I am failing. I have already failed.

I know my parents are worried, but they say nothing to me about Alexander. They never utter a negative word to my face. In our family such things are not talked about. Married couples are expected to work things through on their own without airing their dirty laundry. But I see the worry in their eyes. I hear it in their voices when they talk of benign things.

I pray and I pray for Alexander to know God

and heed Him. We are unequally yoked, to be sure.
I knew we were when I married him. I knew he
had no room for God in his life, but I didn't care.
I ignored the warning voice in my heart. I wanted
to marry Alexander more than I wanted to obey
God. Alexander attended church for a time before
we married, and I told myself that was enough. But
his going to church had nothing to do with faith or
worship or even me. Whatever his reasons for going—to
impress Liza, perhaps?—he never let God come near.

Am I much different? I have sought my own way
again and again.

Mark Thomas turned two yesterday. I was
with Liza and John to help celebrate with cake
and homemade ice cream. Liza has stopped telling
me that someday I will have a child of my own.
She must not want to give me false hope any longer.
Or perhaps she's guessed how seldom my husband
reaches for me in the night.

How much faith do I have? Or what kind of
faith? Am I willing to believe God for my future?
Am I willing to give Alexander and our marriage
over to Him and trust Him to do with it as He
wills?

Last year I decided I needed to discover who
I am. Who I really and truly am as a person, as a
woman, as a Christian. The real me—body, soul, and
spirit. Sometimes I think I know. Sometimes I
think I may never know. I am twenty-three. I've
been a wife for over three years. I've been pregnant
and miscarried. I was with my sister when her
first child passed away, and I was nearby when

she delivered her second child. I can be decisive and brave, but I can also be indecisive and cowardly. I swing from one to the other, as if riding a pendulum.

Should I ask Alexander if he has a mistress? Should I force the issue into the light of day? Or would I rather not have my suspicions confirmed? If I get an answer, I can no longer pretend not to know.

The pendulum swings.

Allison

The nine days her parents stayed with Allison went by in a flash. At the end of their visit, she delivered Gizmo to Susan and then piled into her parents' car and went with them to Seattle to visit her brother and his family and to attend her niece's high school graduation.

As the automobile sped along I-84, Allison couldn't help thinking what a difference a year had made in her life. Last May she'd still been given to fits of tears and periods of feeling blue. Last May her faith had grown cold. Last May she'd felt alone and lonely. Last May she'd felt like a failure—as a woman and as a wife.

"I would have despaired unless I had believed that I would see the goodness of the Lord in the land of the living. Wait for the Lord; be strong and let your heart take courage; yes, wait for the Lord."

As the verses from the Twenty-Seventh Psalm ran through her mind, Allison smiled. She *had* despaired a year ago, but she was learning to be better at waiting on the Lord, at believing she would see His goodness here on earth, at knowing she had already seen it and at counting her blessings. Charles Spurgeon had said a believer must watch for God in the events of life, that one must wait on God with an expectation of His answers. One could not collect the water if no jars were put outside when it rained.

She closed her eyes. *Here are my water jars, Lord. I'm ready for Your rain.*

With a predawn departure and all three of them taking a turn at the wheel, they arrived at Chuck's home in time for supper.

"Allison, you look terrific," her brother said before wrapping her in a bear hug.

When he released her, she replied, "You look pretty good yourself."

Allison and Chuck didn't talk on the phone often or even e-mail with any regularity, but their love for each other wasn't any less real or true. She'd always adored her big brother, and he'd always looked out for her when they were kids. Allison knew she could turn to him anytime for advice or support.

After giving the travelers time to bring in their luggage and wash up, the family sat down to eat. Chuck said a blessing, and then his wife, Joan, began passing around the food.

It was over dessert when Allison said to her niece, "Karen, I can't get over how much you look like your great-grandmother Elizabeth when she was your age. The resemblance is amazing. Have you seen photographs from her wedding? She was eighteen at the time, same as you are now."

"I don't remember seeing any pictures from her wedding." She glanced at her parents. "Have I?"

Chuck shrugged while Joan shook her head.

Allison continued, "I brought a couple of albums along with me, and there's some photos from her wedding. Aunt Emma left a ton of old photos in the attic. I've spent the last year getting them organized into scrapbooks. And if I wasn't flying home, I would have tried to bring all the photos for you to see."

"Allison has done an amazing job," her mother said. "Those photo albums are works of art."

"Thanks, Mom." Pleasure warmed her insides.

Maggie shook a finger at Karen. "And don't you even think

about getting married at your age. You go to college and get your degree first."

"Don't worry, Grandma. I don't even have a boyfriend. I won't be getting married for a long, long time."

"Well, not too long, I hope. I may not want you to rush into marriage, but I would like to attend the weddings of both of my granddaughters." Maggie looked at Allison. "And you can tell Meredith I said so."

When the meal was finished, Joan shooed everyone off to the family room to continue visiting. Everyone but Allison obeyed. She insisted on helping with the cleanup. Besides, it gave the sisters-in-law a chance to talk privately. If Allison had been given a birth sister, she would have wanted her to be like Joan. Chuck's wife had a wicked sense of humor. When in her presence, one needed to be constantly on one's toes. No telling when the next zinger of wit might happen or who would be the recipient.

But tonight Joan didn't seem to be in a joking mood. She sent a serious look in Allison's direction. "Chuck's right." She rinsed dishes and Allison placed them in the dishwasher. "You look good. Straighter. Lighter. Hard to put my finger on it."

"I've lost a few pounds."

"I didn't mean weight, silly."

Allison grinned. "I know you didn't."

"Is it okay to ask . . ." Joan let the words die away.

"About Tony?" Allison finished for her.

Joan nodded.

Allison turned her gaze out the window. "I thought he might die. I really did. More than once. But the last couple of times I've seen him, he looked healthy. He's in a recovery program."

"Do you ever think you two might—"

"Never!"

Joan raised her eyebrows.

"I wouldn't knowingly walk back into that situation."

"But if he stays sober?"

"No." Allison shook her head emphatically. "Not even then. God told me to let go of him and I did." She felt a sting of tears but blinked them back. "Sometimes I think I was the reason he couldn't stay sober."

"What do you mean?"

"I was a soft place to fall."

It was Joan's turn to shake her head.

Allison released a sigh. It was hard to put what she believed into words. "When I *finally* understood what it meant to be co-dependent, to be an enabler and a rescuer, I learned to be pretty good about not doing the obvious things. I didn't clean up after him or put him to bed when he couldn't do it himself. I didn't make excuses to others or cover up with his boss. But even with all of that, if he lost a job, he still had a home. I was still able to pay the bills because of my work. He didn't go homeless or hungry. And I was still trying to be supportive as a wife and not question everything he did. *Trying* being the operative word there. But the truth is, no matter what he did, he didn't truly have to face the consequences of his actions."

"Wow," Joan said softly.

"Yeah. Wow."

"I don't know how you put up with it for so long."

Allison offered a shaky smile. "To tell you the truth, neither do I. I loved Tony. I loved him with all my heart. I wanted our marriage to work. I meant my vows when I said them on our wedding day. For better or worse. I thought tough love would be the answer. I thought God was going to save us." She sighed. "But He didn't."

Allison

Allison's laptop saw little use during her much-too-short visit to Washington. She'd had good intentions when she packed her rolling briefcase, but most of the time she was having far too much fun playing to think about work. Thankfully, she had some leeway with the due dates of her current projects.

Joan, Karen, Maggie, and Allison went into the city on the weekends. They shopped. They saw a touring Broadway show. They shopped some more. They dined in lovely restaurants. They shopped some more and some more after that. And they laughed. A lot. Sometimes Allison's face and sides hurt from all the laughter. She hadn't known she'd needed this mini-vacation until she was in the midst of it.

Attending Karen's high school graduation on the last Thursday in May made the memories whirl inside Allison's head. She thought of her own high school graduation and of Meredith's too. She even recalled the entry Aunt Emma had written after her graduation in May of 1925.

Amazing, how much expectations had changed from then to the present. Especially for girls. Girls in Emma Carter's day rarely considered college as their next step. Most had been more interested in finding the men they would marry or marrying the ones they'd already found. They'd spent more time imagining the homes they would make for their husbands and children than imagining themselves out in the greater world. It hadn't taken Aunt Emma long after she married Alexander Monroe to begin writing in her diary about her desire to become pregnant. Society had thought that was the obvious next step for every young wife. No one thought she should want anything different.

Karen, on the other hand, was both expected and encouraged to continue her education for at least another four years. At eighteen, she was in no rush to marry, settle down, and have a family.

What a cultural shift in less than a hundred years.

It made her wonder what America would be like when her own great-granddaughters and great nieces—should she be blessed with them—came of age. How changed would their world be? How quaint would Allison's life appear to them?

When the two weeks of fun were over—seemingly in a flash—her brother drove her to Sea-Tac for the one-hour flight home to Idaho. She was glad everyone hadn't joined them. She didn't want to blubber curbside as she said more good-byes.

Even with only Chuck to hug before heading into the terminal, she came close to losing control. She blinked back unwelcome tears and said, "You, Joan, and Karen come visit me sometime. Come in the summer and we'll go whitewater rafting. Or horseback riding up in the wilderness area."

"Sounds fun. We'll do it."

"This summer?"

"Don't know that we could do it this year. We're pretty booked for the summer months, and we'll be taking Karen to college in August. Maybe next summer."

Allison kissed his cheek. "Okay then. Whenever you can." She stepped back, grabbed hold of her bags, and smiled. "Keep in touch."

He nodded. "Will do."

She turned and entered the busy interior of the Seattle

airport. It didn't take long to check her large bag and get her boarding pass. Then she headed for the assigned gate, thankful her flight to Boise was less than an hour and a half, gate to gate. She would be back in Kings Meadow and loving on Gizmo well before dark.

Emma

Emma pulled her coat tight and leaned into the bitter February wind. If she didn't hurry, she would be late to work. She'd been employed as a clerk at the small grocery store—ten blocks from her parents' home—since mid-December. The pay wasn't great and sometimes the hours were too long. But with so many people out of work, like Alexander, she was fortunate to have any employment at all.

Most everything she made went to her parents to pay for their board. Her husband didn't like it. He thought the money should go into his pocket, not theirs. Why? So he could spend it on liquor and other women in some speakeasy?

For once Emma had stood her ground. Her wages went to her parents, with a tiny stipend for herself and Alexander. He continued to rail at her whenever her parents were out of hearing, but he hadn't been able to budge her on this. Not on this.

And he hates me for it.

The thought caused her chest to tighten. It was one thing to believe her husband didn't love her, had never loved her. It was another entirely to think he might hate her. Sometimes she wished he would simply take his anger and go away. Leave her. Disappear. Just get in his truck and drive out of sight and never come back. No. No, she didn't wish that. Not really. She'd promised to love, cherish, and obey him until death. She would do exactly that. Divorce had never stained her family. She would not be the first.

But Alexander had made promises too. He'd said he would love and cherish Emma as long as they lived. He'd promised . . . but never meant to keep the promise. He'd never loved or cherished her. Not even briefly. If he'd broken his vows, then couldn't she—

Emma stopped the direction of her thoughts with determination, at the same time quickening her steps. Five minutes later the wind propelled her through the front doorway of the store.

"Merciful heavens!" Mrs. Conners, the proprietress, exclaimed, hurrying over to close the door before it blew nearby items off the shelves. "Have you ever seen such weather?"

"I think it might snow again," Emma answered.

"Indeed."

Emma hung her coat on a hook in the stockroom and slipped a dark apron over her dress. "What would you like me to do today, Mrs. Conners?"

"The shelves could use a good dusting."

"All right."

The gray-haired woman chuckled. "If we left the front door open, it might blow the dust away."

"But what would it blow in?"

"Right you are."

Emma retrieved the feather duster and a cleaning rag and got to work.

Mrs. Conners told her she was going upstairs to check on Mr. Conners who was ailing and would be back shortly. "See to the customers, please. Doubt there'll be any in weather like this, but you never know."

The woman hadn't been gone more than a minute when the front door opened. Emma turned from her tidying and was surprised to see her sister enter the store, Mark Thomas in her arms.

"Liza?"

"I went by the house but you'd already left for work and Mother said Alexander left five minutes after you did. So I came straight here."

Emma felt a flutter of alarm. "Is something wrong?"

"No. On the contrary. John has found a position for Alexander. At a dairy in Meridian."

"A dairy? He's never done that sort of work."

Liza shook her head. "The farmer knows that, but he wants to do John a favor for helping him with some business matter. He's willing to train Alexander."

Emma tried to picture her husband milking cows but couldn't seem to pull up the image.

Shifting her son so he rested on her hip, Liza pulled a folded sheet of paper from her coat pocket and offered it to Emma. "Alexander needs to go see the man today or tomorrow. He mustn't delay or he'll lose the chance."

"I'll tell him as soon as I get home."

"Good. John really wants to help."

"I know."

"He says it's hard on a man to be out of work and unable to provide for his family. It wounds his pride."

Emma wondered if that was true of Alexander. She'd started to think him lazy, without a shred of ambition. But perhaps she'd judged him too harshly. Perhaps—

"Emma?"

"Hmm?"

"If there's anything I can do to help *you* . . ."

Emma saw the pity in her sister's eyes. But she had pride too. She didn't want Liza feeling sorry for her. "This is help enough, Liza. Really."

She'd become almost as good a liar as Alexander.

Allison

June arrived in southwestern Idaho with mild days full of sunshine. Wildflowers splashed an array of colors across hillsides and valleys—white, pink, purple, yellow, blue, red, orange. It made Allison think of an artist's palette, blotches of paint dotting the surface.

With the winter's snowpack long since melted and the ground firm and dry, Allison and Gizmo resumed their afternoon walks along the river. It felt good to stretch her legs after hours at the computer, and the fresh air always managed to clear the to-do list from her congested mind.

Today she found herself wondering how many times in her life Aunt Emma had walked this same path. Had Emma stopped at this particular bend in the river and watched the water tumble, foam, and churn over and around boulders, the way Allison liked to do? How old had Emma been when she came here to live? And what about her husband? What had happened to Alexander Monroe?

The questions teased Allison like a well-tuned mystery novel. She longed to reach the end of the story, but it was also fun to discover the clues along the way.

Allison's first memories of Aunt Emma were here in the mountains. Allison would have been five, maybe six at most. Seen through a child's eyes, the log house had seemed about three times the size it really was. And her aunt had seemed very old even then. She would have been sixty-two or sixty-three. To a little girl, that was ancient.

Aunt Emma had baked chocolate-chip cookies whenever Allison came to visit. That yummy scent had greeted Allison at the door every time. No wonder she'd loved to go visit Aunt Emma!

It made Allison sad to know her aunt's life hadn't always been good, that Emma hadn't been perfectly happy. But whose life was always good? What person on earth got to be happy each and every moment?

Whatever had happened to Aunt Emma, whatever the reason she had for taking back her maiden name and keeping her marriage a secret from later generations, she had made a good life for herself in her log house outside of Kings Meadow. The woman Allison knew had been content, wise, independent, adventurous. Everyone who'd known her had loved and respected her.

It gave Allison hope for her own future. Whatever her past had been, she could decide what her future would be. Choices she made today would determine her tomorrows. Knowing that made her feel stronger than ever before.

The sun was nearly touching the mountaintops in the west by the time Allison and Gizmo left the path along the river and climbed the incline toward the highway. They weren't quite to the top when Allison saw a black pickup truck—the same kind as about twenty others in the area—turn off the road into her driveway.

"Come on, Gizmo. We've got company."

They quickened their pace.

By the time the house came into view, the driver was out of the truck and up on the deck. She didn't have to get closer to know who it was. Chet Leonard.

"I think he likes you." The memory of her mom's comment made her suddenly nervous.

Chet turned away from the door, started toward the steps, saw her, stopped, and waved.

She waved back.

"Hey, stranger," he called to her, grinning. "How was your vacation? Susan says you had a great time in Seattle."

"I did, but it's good to be home." She climbed the steps to the deck. "What brings you out here?"

He removed his Stetson and bent down to greet Gizmo with a few strokes on the head. As he straightened, he answered, "It's time I got my business online and quit relying on the newspapers to sell my horses. I hear tell you're the person I need to see about it."

"I'd be glad to help you, Chet." *See, Mom. It's just business.* "Come on inside." She unlocked the door. "Would you like some iced tea? I need something to drink after my walk."

"Sure."

"Lemon?"

"Please."

She took the pitcher from the refrigerator, filled two large glasses with tea, and added lemon wedges to the rims. As she handed a glass to Chet, she said, "There's sugar and sweetener packets on the table."

He squeezed the juice from the lemon into the tea. "This should be fine." He took a sip. "Hits the spot."

"Come on out to the living room. We'll talk about what you want. Just give me a sec while I grab a few things from my office." She went into the bedroom and picked up her laptop, a spiral notebook, and a pen.

By the time Allison got to the living room, Chet had settled in one of the matching chairs near the window. Allison had bought the set earlier in the year. The chairs were mauve in color and smallish, made for a woman's more delicate frame. Chet Leonard was anything but delicate, and he seemed to dwarf the furniture. She nearly laughed aloud at the sight.

As if reading her mind, he stood. "Maybe the sofa would be better . . . so I can see your laptop if you want to show me something."

"I think so."

Her mother's voice seemed to whisper in her ear a second time: "*I think he likes you.*"

Silently, Allison answered, *Be quiet. Go away.*

But her mother never had been one to let go of anything related to love and romance—or the possibility of same—not even in her daughter's imagination.

More than an hour later Allison and Chet rose from the sofa.

"Thanks for giving me so much of your time." He picked up his Stetson and held it in his right hand. "It's pretty obvious I'm still living in the dark ages."

Allison laughed. "Not quite that bad."

"You're being kind."

"Maybe a little."

"Don't think you'll insult me if you speak the truth. My boys have a way of letting me know how far I am behind the times."

They walked toward the door and stepped outside onto the deck. Dusk had settled over the forest and the air had cooled.

Chet stopped at the top of the stairs and set his hat on his head. "If I had my druthers, we'd all be riding horses, corresponding with pen and paper, and having face-to-face conversations over supper."

"You'd want to give up that fancy four-wheel drive pickup of yours?"

"Well . . . maybe not my pickup." He grinned and winked.

The wink made her stomach feel funny.

Chet started down the steps. "See you in church," he called over his shoulder.

"Yes. See you there."

He strode to the truck, opened the door, then stopped and turned around. "Hey, would you like to come out to the ranch tomorrow after church? You could have lunch with me and the boys, and we could show you around the place. Might help you get a feel for what we do."

There was that funny feeling in her stomach again.

"Maybe Susan and Ned could come too," he added.

No reason to feel funny. It wasn't like he was asking her on a date. "Sounds like a good idea. Mind if Gizmo tags along?"

"Nope. He'll be welcome too."

Allison remained on the deck, her dog sitting by her right leg, and watched as Chet got in his truck, started the engine, turned the pickup around, and drove away.

Allison

The next afternoon Allison leaned against the top rail of a wooden fence and stared across the rolling pastureland of the Leonard ranch. To the north, rugged mountains formed a gorgeous backdrop. Horses—dozens of them—grazed or slept in fields of green. In a paddock off to her right, a palomino rolled on his back, stirring up a dust cloud. The air smelled of newly mown lawn and hay.

This was why people wanted the life of a cowboy. Or at least to live in close proximity to cowboys.

"Beautiful, isn't it?" Chet stepped up beside her.

"Beautiful." She turned and leaned her back against the fence, her gaze moving to the barn and the two-story house beyond.

Chet's two boys were throwing a Frisbee for Gizmo in the fenced backyard while Ned and Susan Lyle observed them from the covered patio.

Last summer, when Marsha was still here and Rick was still living, the Leonards had invited Allison to come out to the ranch on a couple of different occasions. For one reason or another, she hadn't been able to accept. Now she regretted it. There was something restful about this place.

"My great-granddad ran cattle on our land in the early part of the last century," he said. "It was my grandpa who made the move to raising quarter horses." He motioned with his head toward the paddocks behind the barn. "Some great performance horses have come out of this place. Lots of champions. Cutting. Barrels. You name it. Likely one of ours has done it."

"Do you rodeo?"

He shook his head. "Not anymore. Did when I was younger. Before the kids came. But all that traveling around wasn't what I wanted for my family. I wanted to be a hands-on kind of dad. Be here when they took their first steps and all the firsts that followed."

"Too bad there aren't more fathers like you."

"What about your ex-husband? Was he a good dad?"

She was surprised by the question.

"Sorry. Too personal? I shouldn't have asked."

"No. It's all right. But it isn't easy to answer. It's complicated."

"Life's complicated." Chet turned his gaze toward the mountains.

"Tony was a good dad, most of the time. He loved our daughter. But sometimes . . ." She let her voice trail away.

"Marsha was a good mom to our boys. I guess we had our troubles like any married couple, but we always worked through them. But after Rick died . . . Well, I guess there were more cracks in the foundation of our marriage than I knew. Never would've dreamed she'd take off the way she did. Leave our sons. Get a divorce. Cut herself off completely from her past and everyone she knows and loves."

Softly, Allison said, "Our situation wasn't quite the same, but Tony walked out too. It's a unique kind of hurt, being abandoned by the one you love."

"I'm sorry. I didn't know."

"No reason you would have."

"How long was it before you stopped feeling like your lungs were being crushed?"

She figured that was a rhetorical question. And even if not, she wasn't sure she could answer it. So she simply laid a hand on his upper arm.

Emma

1931

Emma hurried toward the house she and Alexander had moved into in the spring. Despite her best efforts to make them look otherwise, the three rooms were small and gloomy. Nothing she did made the house feel like a home. But Alexander had insisted after working at the dairy for a few months that they move out of her parents' home, and the three-room stucco was all they could afford.

Alexander had seemed in a better mood over the summer. He laughed more. His words were kinder. He'd even gone to church with her a few times in August. They seemed to be friends again. Emma liked that and let hope blossom in her heart. Alexander had even agreed to go with her to Mark Thomas's birthday party tonight. Her nephew was three years old, and the cutest little boy in the world.

She felt a pinch of sadness, a longing for a baby of her own. Especially now that Liza was pregnant again. How many prayers had Emma sent winging toward heaven, begging God to give her a child to love? Hundreds? Thousands? Was His answer no or not yet?

She glanced at her wristwatch. Mrs. Conners had let her off work an hour ahead of schedule so she would have ample time to change her clothes and freshen her hair before Alexander got home from the dairy. Even so, it would be difficult to make the party on time.

Please don't let Alexander forget about tonight. Don't let him be late getting home.

Unlike her prayers for a baby, this one was answered quickly. When she turned the corner and looked toward the end of the block, she saw her husband's truck in the driveway. Alexander hadn't forgotten. He'd not only remembered, but he'd gotten home before her. Smiling, she quickened her steps.

She entered the house through the kitchen door. It only took a few steps to carry her across the room to the bedroom door. As she turned the knob, she said, "Alexander."

In that moment her world came crashing to a halt.

Her husband was in bed—and he wasn't alone.

"Emma, what are you doing home?"

It was as if she could see herself from afar. Her eyes widened. One hand gripped the doorjamb. The breath caught in her chest. Her face paled. A buzzing sound filled her ears.

"Emma."

She turned away, went into the parlor, too confused to know what to do next. Her stomach rolled and she thought she might be sick. Time passed as she stood in the middle of the room, powerless to move, unable to think.

"Emma."

She turned toward Alexander, who stood framed in the archway between the parlor and kitchen. He wore trousers but no shirt. His feet were bare.

"What are you doing home?" he asked again, scowling at her.

Somehow words came out of her mouth. "Mark Thomas's party is tonight."

He muttered a curse.

"Who is she?" Emma whispered.

"It doesn't matter."

"I'm your wife. It matters to me."

But did it? Did it really matter who that woman was? It wasn't as if Emma hadn't known he'd been unfaithful in the past. Did it matter the name of the strumpet he'd brought into their bed? Was *she* the reason he'd seemed happier of late?

That thought sparked something inside of Emma. A rage she hadn't known it was possible to feel. "You brought her into *my* home! Into *our* bed!" She took two quick steps forward and slapped him.

She had no time at all to prepare for his reaction. The back of his hand struck her with such fury she flew backward, hitting the wall. Pain exploded in her head. Air gushed from her lungs. Then she screamed as he moved toward her, murder in his eyes.

Allison

Something unexpected happened to Allison during the weeks that followed. She became aware of herself as a woman again. She hadn't realized the awareness was gone until it came back to her. She found herself looking at men and wondering if they were single. Which appalled her to no end. But Meredith found it funny when Allison confessed the realization to her one evening over the telephone.

"Why wouldn't you wonder about single men, Mom? You're not dead yet."

"I know that, honey, but I'm not interested in men. Not in any romantic kind of way. I'm never getting married again, so what point is there in it?"

"Bet that drives Grandma crazy when she hears it."

Allison leaned back in the deck chair and stared up at the soft blue-gray sky. "You have no idea."

"Sure I do. Grandma can't wait to get me married off. She's always asking if I've met someone special."

"Well? Have you?"

"Mom!"

Allison grinned. "Couldn't help myself. And there was someone you liked last year. What happened to him?"

"Didn't go anywhere. Hey, before I forget, have you talked to Dad lately?"

"No." Out of habit, her stomach clenched. "Why?"

"I'm going to use my vacation time to come visit you both, but I really hate having to divide time between Boise and Kings Meadow. The time goes by so fast as it is."

Disappointment replaced wariness. Allison was greedy enough to want Meredith with her the entire time.

"Would it be all right with you if Dad came to stay at your place for those two weeks? He's got vacation time coming too."

Allison opened her mouth, intending to refuse, but something stopped her. She wasn't sure what. Perhaps because she always found it hard to refuse her daughter. Or was it something else?

"We got along great at Christmas, the three of us," Meredith added, not knowing the battle was won.

"You're right. We did."

"Could you take some time off from your work so we could do a bit of traveling? Maybe go camping at Redfish Lake."

"When are you coming?" Allison headed inside to check her schedule on the computer.

"Around Labor Day, if that works for you. I'm thinking the week before and the one after."

Allison looked through her planner, estimating in her head. "Yes," she said at last. "I could do *some* traveling with you. Couldn't be gone the whole two weeks, though."

Even as she said it, she knew once Meredith arrived, it would be the same as when she visited her brother in May. She would play instead of sitting down to work. Her desk and computer would gather dust until her daughter went back to Texas. But that was okay. She would just have to put in extra hours in the first weeks of August so she wouldn't feel guilty during Meredith's visit.

And Tony's visit.

"Mom? Did you hear what I said?"

"No. I'm sorry. I let my mind wander. What was it?"

"I said I'll firm up the dates of my vacation and then let Dad know so he can do the same. I'll be in touch as soon as I have particulars, like my flight times and such."

"Okay."

They exchanged a few more words and then ended the call.

As Allison put down the handset, she wondered what she was doing, letting Tony come to stay a second time. When she saw him in April, he'd made her angry. Angry and confused because he'd manipulated her feelings. That was how it had seemed anyway. Would seeing him again, letting him stay in the spare room, bring those unwelcome feelings back?

When Tony was out of sight, he was out of mind. When he was out of mind, Allison's life was easier. In these mountains she didn't have as many reminders of him and the life they'd had, both good and bad. A few memories but not many. Not constant. She was certain that was why God brought her there to live. So she could heal. So she could move on. The Lord had told Allison to let go, and she had, though sometimes it seemed He'd pried her clutching fingers loose one stubborn digit at a time.

Emma

1931

"Emma?" Liza's voice was loud and clear from the other side of the front door. "Emma, open the door." She knocked again.

Emma leaned her back against the wall, holding her breath, as if afraid her sister would hear her breathing. She didn't want Liza to see her today. Not like this. Not with her face swollen and bruises on her arms and legs.

"Emma, I am not leaving until you open this door. I know something is wrong."

Make her go away. Please make her go away.

"Please, Em." Liza's voice softened. "Please. I will stand here all day if I must. Or I'll send for someone to break down the door."

Liza would do it too.

Exhaling a breath of defeat, Emma pushed away from the wall and crossed the living room. She stood there for a few moments, fingertips on the knob. Finally, she opened the door, her gaze locked on the floor.

"Em—" Liza gasped, then she whispered, "Saints alive. What has he done to you?"

Tears blurred Emma's vision. Her throat was too tight to speak. Her face hurt. Her body hurt. But it was the emptiness in her heart that was the worst of all.

Liza entered the house. "Alexander's at the dairy?"

Emma nodded.

"Good. Get your things. Get whatever is important because whatever you leave behind you leave for good. You are never coming back to this house again."

Never coming back?

Liza reached out to touch Emma's cheek, then drew her hand back, as if afraid she might cause her more pain. "What sort of monster would hurt you this way?"

Out of habit, Emma wanted to leap to Alexander's defense. She wanted to say he wasn't as bad as Liza thought. She wanted to say he loved her. She wanted to believe things would be better tomorrow. But she couldn't. She couldn't say anything, and she hadn't any strength left to believe in a lie.

While Emma remained immobilized by the front door, Liza sprang into action. She went into the bedroom, flung open the top of Emma's hope chest, and began filling it with clothes from the small chest of drawers.

Never coming back.

"When you didn't come for Mark Thomas's party and you didn't send word or call, I knew it was something like this." Liza practically threw the items into the chest. "Has he hit you before?" She stopped and stared sadly at Emma.

She shook her head and mouthed the word *no*.

"I never did know what you saw in him, Emma. I never understood why you liked him in the first place. Oh, he's handsome and charming. No one could deny that, but he's a scoundrel, through and through."

"No, he—"

"He drinks. He flirts. He's thoughtless and selfish. And he's been unfaithful, hasn't he?"

The memory of yesterday afternoon flashed in Emma's head—the woman in bed with Alexander, how he'd blamed

Emma for it, the first blow as it connected with her cheek. "He's my husband," she whispered.

"Not for long, he's not." Liza turned to the chest. "Is that everything you want?"

Emma shook her head. "No." She went to the cabinet in the living room where she kept her journals. There were six of them now, representing nine years of her life. She gathered them into her arms and took them to the bedroom, dropping them into the chest. Afterward, she removed a framed photograph from the wall, the one of her and Alexander on their wedding day, and added it to the chest. Liza raised her eyebrows over that, but Emma ignored her as she went to retrieve a shoebox of photographs and a few more personal items. When she couldn't think of another thing she would need or want, Emma put on a hat with a veil, hoping to hide her face from any watchful eyes. Then each of them took hold of an end handle on the cedar chest and they carried it outside to Liza's automobile.

By the time Emma was settled into the passenger seat, she was exhausted. Where would she find the strength to go through the days ahead? How many people would have to know what Alexander had done to her? Would the identity of that woman in Emma's bed come to light? Emma had suspected he'd been unfaithful, had known it in her heart. But she'd never imagined he would bring his floozies into their home. How he must hate her to do something like that.

Liza turned to look at her. "John and I will help you every step along the way. You can stay with us for as long as you need. We'll protect you."

"I don't want Father and Mother to see me like this. They can't know about it. It's too . . . too humiliating."

"They'll have to be told you've left Alexander and why you're getting a divorce."

Divorce. The word was black and cold and hopeless. Shame coursed through Emma. Whatever the reasons her husband couldn't love her, whatever the reasons for his unfaithfulness, whatever the reasons he'd become angry enough to strike her, he had never mentioned divorce. And he hadn't always been unkind or thoughtless or cruel. There had been good moments in their marriage. Hadn't there?

The ache in her chest became too intense to bear, and she began to weep.

"Sis," Liza said softly but with steel in her voice, "marriage does not give a man the right to beat his wife. A husband is supposed to love her so much he would die for her, like Christ for the church."

Emma turned her face away, staring out the passenger window at a world that seemed remote, distant, unreal.

Surely she would never be happy again.

Allison

The Lyles held a barbecue on the Fourth of July—an annual event. Friends and neighbors from all over the area were in attendance. The backyard teemed with people.

What surprised Allison was how different she felt this year from last year. Last year she'd been a newcomer, a stranger, an outsider. *A flatlander*, she thought with a smile.

At the moment, she was alone in Susan's large kitchen. She lifted the lid of the cooler she'd brought from home and took out the last container of ambrosia salad she'd contributed to the barbecue. She popped off the lid and scooped the yummy mixture into several smaller serving bowls. To brighten the salad, she added maraschino cherries to the top.

This had been her great-aunt's go-to recipe for picnics. Allison remembered standing on a stool in the kitchen—before it had been modernized—Aunt Emma watching as Allison mixed the marshmallows, sour cream, mandarin oranges, pineapple, and coconut together in a bowl. Dear Aunt Emma. In the memory, she had a cap of curly gray hair and she wore large round eyeglasses, so fashionable back in the eighties.

Allison continued to read the journals, although not as quickly as she would like. Her pleasure-reading time had been limited as of late due to an especially difficult-to-please client who shot off a barrage of e-mails that Allison had to answer every day of the week. The client kept changing her mind about what she wanted, and finding the right design was like trying to shoot a moving duck. Bless her.

This past week she'd reached her aunt's entry from October 1928, the one about her miscarriage. The miscarriage that had come the day after Emma's nephew's birth. Mark Thomas Hendricks. Allison's Uncle Mark. Her mother's big brother. Allison had never met Uncle Mark. He'd died in the Korean War at the age of twenty-two or twenty-three. Since he'd never been a part of her life, she'd never given him much thought. But reading Aunt Emma's diary made the experiences of that generation of her family feel so much more personal to her. Made her realize the hurts and triumphs they'd gone through.

How much do I not know about Mom, let alone Grandma and Aunt Emma? What does Mom keep secret from me, even today?

In recent months Allison had asked a number of older residents of the valley if they knew what year Emma Carter moved to the house outside of Kings Meadow. None could say for sure. Allison had then tried researching tax records, but a fire at the county courthouse many years before had destroyed the information she sought. It seemed she would have to wait for the answer until she read about it in an entry in one of the upcoming journals. And as tempting as it was to jump ahead, she was compelled to wait. She was discovering more than mere facts as she read the diaries. She felt as if she'd met a different woman from the one she'd believed she knew so well. She was convinced that if Aunt Emma could survive loss and an unhappy marriage, if she could blossom from the uncertain young woman and wife of these early entries into the amazing older woman Allison had known and loved, then maybe there was hope for her. Maybe—

"Are you hiding in here?"

She looked up to find Chet Leonard framed in the kitchen doorway.

"Need any help?" he asked without waiting for her to answer his first question.

"Yes." She lifted two of the serving bowls. "You can carry these outside for me."

He grinned. "Glad to." He reached for them.

Allison picked up the remaining bowl and followed Chet out onto the deck and down the steps to the back lawn. Two long tables, borrowed from the Methodist church, had been placed in the shade to the right of the patio. Pale smoke rose from the grill where Ned cooked more hamburgers and hot dogs for the still-hungry crowd.

As he set down the serving bowls, Chet said, "Did I tell you I've already made a couple of sales because of the new website?"

"No, you didn't."

"Can't thank you enough for what you did." He cocked one eyebrow. "Are you sure you charged me enough?"

It was true she hadn't charged him her usual fee, but she'd charged him enough. She answered him truthfully, "I'm sure."

He hesitated a moment, then said, "I don't suppose you'd care to go with me to a movie sometime."

Was he asking her out? On a date?

"We can wait until there's something playing you'd really like to see. But I hear there're some good ones out." He cocked an eyebrow. "Maybe one day next week?"

A shiver of nerves passed along her spine as she nodded. She hadn't been on a date in forever.

"Midweek okay? Next Wednesday? We could leave early enough to have dinner first."

"Okay." Gracious! What would her mother and Meredith have to say about this unexpected development? Well, unexpected for Allison. Not so much for her mother.

"I'll call you tomorrow."

"Okay," she repeated.

He took a step away. "I'd better go spell Ned at the grill. You staying for the fireworks?"

"Yes."

His smile broadened, and the nerves erupted in her stomach this time.

Meredith's words whispered in Allison's memory: *"You're not dead yet."*

Apparently not.

Allison

Allison inspected her reflection. She'd received her dark hair and olive complexion from her dad's side of the family. But she hoped she'd inherited her mom's youthful complexion. Grandma Elizabeth had still been a stunning beauty at the age of eighty—oh, her flawless skin!—and Aunt Emma had looked a good two decades younger than her years well into her nineties.

Allison turned sideways toward the mirror. She liked the look of her figure since losing a few more pounds. Ten or twelve of them since last year. All of her walks with Gizmo on these mountain trails had paid a nice bonus.

But she wished she were more creative about how to wear her shoulder-length hair. Her hair stylist in Boise had wanted to experiment, but Allison always put her off. Besides, when her hair didn't play nice, she could capture it in a ponytail and forget it. And that was what she'd done today. A ponytail said, *Casual, not serious. We're just friends. Dinner and a movie isn't anything to be nervous about.* But that wasn't what the butterflies in her stomach said.

Gizmo barked, letting Allison know Chet had arrived. She grabbed her sweater off the foot of the bed. The heat of summer had come to the forest, but the sweater would be welcome when the chill of night returned. She went out onto the deck, locking the door behind her. There was no breeze today, and the towering lodgepole pines were dead still. Dust swirled in front of Chet's truck after he brought it to a halt.

"You're ready, I see," he called to her.

"I'm ready." She went down the steps.

Chet hurried around the pickup to open the door for her. "You look nice." He offered a hand to help her into the cab.

He looked good too, but she didn't tell him so. "Thank you, Mr. Leonard. Your mama trained you well."

"She did, indeed, Ms. Kavanagh." He grinned.

How strange this all seemed. She was forty-six but she felt fourteen. Awkward and unsure. Her mother would be delighted to know Allison was going out with a nice man. Meredith would be pleased too. But whatever God's opinion, He'd chosen to be silent for now. At least, Allison hadn't heard an answer to her prayers about this night. She didn't sense His disapproval, but neither did she sense that this was a doorway He wanted her to walk through.

Chet got in behind the wheel and turned his truck around. "Care for some music? I've got Brad Paisley in the CD player."

She squinted at the slot in the console. "Really. I wouldn't have thought he was thin enough to fit in there."

Chet laughed.

Allison felt both imprudent and guilty. It was the kind of thing she and Tony used to say to each other after one of them opened the doorway for a zinger. It felt wrong to say it to someone else. It felt . . . fickle.

Chet must have taken her silence as consent for he turned on the music, setting the volume low enough to allow for comfortable conversation.

After about a mile, Allison asked about his boys.

"Sam's struggled in school this year. Not sure if it's being fifteen or if it's having his folks get divorced or if it's Rick's death. Probably a combination of all that. Pete's doing a little better than his brother. Both of them are in counseling with Pastor

Josh. I think that's helped them navigate these rough waters better than they would have otherwise."

"And you?"

"Most days I'm navigating okay. I never pictured myself as divorced."

"I know what you mean. Neither did I."

His hands tightened on the steering wheel. "When we're young, we don't realize how complicated life can get. I thought that as long as I loved God and tried to walk the straight and narrow nothing bad would come my way. Naive, wasn't I? Certainly I never thought anything like the death of a child or my wife walking out the way she did would happen." He glanced at Allison, then back at the road. "I'm luckier than many. I've got a good group of Christian men to lean on. Got a good pastor to talk to when I can't make sense of my feelings."

"And none of your friends had to choose between you and Marsha."

He gave her another quick look. "Is that what happened to you?"

"Yes. Good friends don't mean for that to happen, of course. They try to stay friends with both parties in a divorce. But it rarely works out that way."

"Do you mind if I ask why you and your husband split up?"

"I don't mind talking about it." But before the words *Tony is an alcoholic* could come out of her mouth, they seemed to lodge in her throat. Plenty of times during the year they were separated she'd told others about her husband's problems. Even before. But now that Tony was doing well in recovery, it felt wrong to speak of it. Maybe not to tell a close friend and spiritual mentor like Susan, but definitely wrong in this situation. "But it's rather complicated. Like you said."

He was a true gentleman, changing the subject to something

benign and nonthreatening. "What kind of food do you want to eat? We've got lots of choices when we get down to the city. Not like in Kings Meadow."

No wonder she liked this cowboy.

Emma

October 5, 1931

That man came to Liza's house today. Mr. Smith. The bootlegger Alexander works for. He was looking for Alexander. He wanted to know where he is. I had nothing to tell him. I do not know where he is. How could I? I do not think he believed me.

After he left, I had no choice but to tell Liza about Alexander's illegal activities. I think this surprised her more than anything that has happened. And I think it frightened her too. She told me I am not to answer the door again. I cannot blame her.

It would upset her even more should I confess that I still love Alexander, despite everything. She thinks love should have died with the first blow. I would have thought so too. But it did not die. My heart is broken. I thought nothing would ever hurt me as much as losing our baby, but this hurts every bit as much. This is a death of a different kind, but still a death.

God, I am afraid of what tomorrow will bring. I went from my father's house to my husband's house. I have never been anything other than a daughter or a wife. I do not want to go back to depending upon my parents to care for me. But what else can I do?

Able-bodied men cannot get jobs, and I cannot live on the little I earn from the grocery. Please tell me what to do, Father. You tell us not to fear, but I am afraid anyway.

I am twenty-four, but I feel so much older. Sometimes I feel ancient. Dried up. As if a strong wind could blow me away and I would exist no more.

Why couldn't you love me, Alexander? Why did it have to end this way?

Allison

The following Sunday Chet asked Allison if she would like to sit with him and the boys in church. She agreed, although she knew people would talk. She treasured the community of believers who made up Meadow Fellowship, but like every church, large or small, it had its share of gossips. She decided not to let that stop her from accepting Chet's invitation.

The truth was, she liked him. She liked him a lot. And despite all of her nerves last Wednesday, she'd had a good time. They'd visited about a wide range of topics during their drive to and from Boise, as well as over dinner at a steakhouse. They'd both enjoyed the movie and, afterward, discussed how it differed from the book. And when they arrived at her home, he walked her to the door, waited while she let Gizmo out, and only when he knew she was safely inside for the night did he return to his truck and leave.

When the service was over that morning, Chet invited her to join him and the boys for a bite to eat at the restaurant in town. Although she was tempted to accept, she decided she'd given the gossips enough fodder for one day and declined.

At home, she watered the flowers in boxes and pots on the front deck as well as the ones planted alongside the house in the backyard. Early in the summer she'd had a fence installed in the back to help protect Gizmo from bears and coyotes. Still, she kept a watchful eye on him as he ran around the yard.

Once inside, Allison changed into cropped pants and a T-shirt, then she made herself a tuna fish sandwich for lunch. When she was finished eating, she decided to make the afternoon a true time of rest. She went into the bedroom, grabbed the latest leather journal, and headed for the sofa in the living room. With a comfortable pillow behind her head and a light throw across her legs, she opened the diary and began to read.

November 3, 1928

Why is it time seems to pass so quickly when I am happy and it creeps along when there is sorrow in my life?

I have decided, of all the things I am told to do as a Christian, to pray, "Thy will be done" is the most difficult. How do I pray it and mean it when I know God's will may be for me to go through more trials, through more fire? I do not like the fire.

I went to see Liza and little Mark Thomas today. Holding the baby in my arms, I felt as if something died inside of me along with the baby I lost. Mark Thomas is so adorable. Even more so at four weeks old than on the day of his birth a month ago. Would his cousin have looked like him? Would they have been the best of friends? I cannot know.

Liza no longer seems like my little sister. She used to be such a flirt, a flibbertigibbet, her head full of boys, boys, boys. Now, at twenty, there is a maturity in her I wondered if I would ever see. Serene. That is the word I would use to describe her. I used to watch out for Liza. Now I feel her trying to watch out for me. But what can she do? I must find the courage within to face the world as it is. I must learn to be a good wife to Alexander, no matter what tomorrow brings. I must learn to be a faithful follower of Jesus, forgiving those who hurt me and not holding on so tightly to those things I want or think I deserve.

This morning I read this about Abraham in the fourth chapter of Romans: "And being not weak in faith, he considered not his own body now dead, when he was about an hundred years old, neither yet the deadness of Sarah's womb: He staggered not at the promise of God through unbelief; but was strong in faith, giving glory to God; And being fully persuaded that, what he had promised, he was able also to perform."

It occurred to me Abraham saw himself, saw his wife, as they really were and still believed God would keep His promise. I cannot pretend I am different than I am. I cannot pretend my life is different than it is. I must see the truth and trust God in the midst of it. Despite it.

Help me, Father, to do that. Amen.

Allison closed the journal. Something had shifted in her chest as she read the last of the entry. It was as if the truth slapped her on the forehead and shouted, "Pay attention!" How often had she pretended her life was well and rosy rather than accept reality and deal with it? How often had she failed to trust God when things were at their bleakest, as if He hadn't been right there with her?

Too often.

Aunt Emma had been half Allison's age when she wrote those words, but she'd been wiser, even then.

But the shift inside Allison wasn't about her aunt. Not really. It wasn't about wisdom or ignorance, youth or maturity. She sensed God teaching her something through it. Or at least He was using the diaries to get her attention. She closed her eyes, straining to hear Him, wanting to understand completely, not satisfied with bits and pieces of understanding.

The walk of a Christian, Allison had learned, was just that. A walk. A conscious action. Setting her face in a certain direction and moving forward with resolve. If—when—she stopped moving forward, she didn't stand still. She went backward, like someone facing the wrong way on a conveyor belt.

Which am I doing? Moving forward or sliding backward? Am I believing You, God, for the future?

No answers came, and a short while later Allison drifted off to sleep.

Emma

1932

It was a gray, drizzling afternoon in March when Liza, large with child, waddled into the bedroom and found Emma clutching her wedding photo to her chest and weeping. "That's enough, Emma," she said sternly. "Enough."

"I can't help it."

"Yes, you can. Get off of that bed. Wash your face and fix your hair. Change your clothes. Stop feeling sorry for yourself. You aren't the first woman to be divorced, and divorce isn't the unforgivable sin. Get up and go for a walk. Look at the world. Count your blessings."

"It's raining out."

"A bit of rain won't hurt you."

Liza didn't understand. Liza had everything she'd ever wanted. A husband who loved her. A healthy son and another baby soon to be born. Although not as rich as they once were, the Hendricks family wasn't poor and destitute as so many were in these troubled times. As Emma was. Liza had a beautiful home and plenty of food on the table and could still afford to keep a couple of servants. Emma had nothing but emptiness and loneliness. It shamed her, this blanket of self-pity she wore like a cloak, but she couldn't seem to crawl out from under it. She'd tried but she couldn't. Her thoughts returned again and again to her life with Alexander, to what they might have had, to actions she might have taken to make a difference before everything went wrong.

Emma turned her face toward the wall. "Go away. I want to be alone."

"I will not go away." Unexpectedly, Liza grabbed the framed photograph and jerked it free of Emma's grip, then took several steps backward. "You cannot go on like this. It isn't healthy. Look at you. You're thin and wan. You have no care for your appearance. This isn't like you, Em."

Emma wanted to take her photograph back, but she hadn't the energy to do so.

Liza's expression softened a little. "Em, please. Don't let that man continue to hurt you like this. That's all you're doing. Letting him go on hurting you."

"He was my husband. I promised to stay with him unto death."

"And he promised to love and cherish you. Didn't he? Was it love when he went off with other women? Was it love when he struck you?"

Emma's breath caught and she mouthed the word *no*. Then she held out a hand, silently asking for the return of her photograph. It was the only one she had from their wedding day. She had other snapshots of Alexander, even a few of the two of them together, but the one Liza now held was the only one from their wedding day.

The unspoken request seemed to make her sister angry all over again. With a suddenness that shocked Emma, Liza removed the photograph from its frame and ripped it into tiny pieces. The action sucked the air from the room. Neither woman moved as the last bits of the torn photograph drifted to the floor.

"What have you done?" Emma whispered after a lengthy silence.

"I hope I've brought you to your senses. I'm sorry, Emma, but enough is enough. It's time you rejoined the world of the living." With that, Liza left the room as quickly as her pregnant body allowed.

Emma got off the bed, knelt on the floor, and picked up the remains of her wedding picture. There was no hope of gluing it back together again. The pieces were too small, the rips too uneven.

Liza's right. Get up. Move on.

But she remained on her knees, feeling as if more than a photograph had been shredded. Her heart, too, lay in pieces on the hardwood floor.

Allison

Chet invited Allison for dinner or coffee at least once each week in the month that followed their first date. She accepted because she enjoyed his company—and yet it disturbed her too. She had a feeling Chet would like a more serious relationship, at least down the road a bit. What she wanted remained a mystery to her.

Chet never tried to kiss her. He never did anything more intimate than place his hand in the small of her back as they entered a restaurant. But there was something about the way he looked at her that told her the time would come.

Why wasn't she eager for romance to happen? She thought she should be. Her mother and her daughter thought she should be as well. And yet something held her emotions in check. Something that said she wasn't ready for more than Chet's friendship. It was frustrating, really. He was one of the nicest men she'd ever known. A good dad. A strong Christian. And the two of them had many things in common, including knowing what it was like to be abandoned by a spouse, to be divorced against their wills.

It was a hot afternoon in mid-August when Allison decided to share her confused emotions with Susan. The two women sat in the shade on the deck, cool glasses of iced tea in their hands. Allison talked and talked. Susan listened without comment until Allison ran out of words.

"Well," she said into the sudden silence.

"Well," Allison echoed in a whisper.

"You know Chet is a dear, dear friend of ours. Ned's and mine."

"Of course."

"And though we may have known you for a shorter period of time, you are just as dear a friend to us."

Allison smiled briefly in acknowledgment.

"I am not surprised you and Chet hit it off. In other circumstances, you might have been ideal for each other."

In other circumstances.

"Maybe that time will still come." Susan leaned forward on her chair. "But have you considered the reason you aren't ready for romance, as you put it, is because God doesn't want you to be ready for it?"

"Why would that be?"

"My friend, the older I get, the more I realize how little I know. None of us are good at waiting on God. Our culture wants instant everything. Even up here in these mountains, where life is less rushed than in the cities, we still can be impatient with life. We don't want to wait. We want what we want and we want it now. The television tells us we are worthy of whatever will make us beautiful or rich or smart or happy, and we want it. But the only real answer to your question is wait. Wait and pray. Pray and listen. God will answer you in His time."

"Mm." Allison leaned back in her chair and looked up at the sky, watching the tall pines sway gently. "I *have* prayed about it. Did I tell you I've been journaling more? Like Aunt Emma, I've been writing out my prayers. It helps me to see them on the page."

"Then perhaps that's where God will answer you. On the pages of your journal."

Allison liked the sound of that.

After a brief silence, Susan asked, "When is Meredith arriving?"

"Saturday after next."

"You must be excited."

"I am. It feels like ages since she was here, even though it's only been seven months. I miss her terribly."

"Of course you do."

Allison cast a glance toward her friend. "There's something I haven't told you about this visit to Idaho."

"What's that?"

"Tony's coming with her."

"Really?" Susan raised an eyebrow but she didn't sound surprised.

"He'll stay in the exercise room on that blow-up bed, like he did for Christmas. And the three of us might go camping up at Redfish Lake for a few nights. That's what Meredith wants to do."

Susan laughed softly. "You are an unusual ex-wife, Allison Kavanagh."

"Do you think so?"

"You feel no bitterness after all that's happened?"

"No."

"Did you ever?"

Allison didn't answer as quickly this time. She considered the question, wanting to be honest with Susan and with herself. Finally, she said, "No, I was never bitter. Heartbroken, yes. Bitter, no. Tony was never a bad man. Alcoholism made him selfish, of course. He could hurt my feelings. He hurt me deeply at times. And I could get angry. Terribly angry. I could strike back with words meant to wound. I'm ashamed of those times."

"You still care about him." Susan didn't phrase it as a question.

Care for Tony? Yes, she did care about him. She and Tony had lived together for more than two decades. They'd brought a child into the world and raised her together. They'd fought and they'd cried. They'd laughed and they'd loved. Divorce couldn't negate the memories, good or bad. She might not love him any longer, but she could still care about him, about his health, his recovery, his walk with God. She could still want the best for him.

Perhaps Susan was right. Perhaps Allison was an unusual ex-wife.

Allison

During the week before Meredith arrived, Allison put in long hours at the computer, making certain she was ahead of schedule on her current projects. When she wasn't doing that, she cleaned and organized like a mad woman. The exercise room was less cluttered than it had been at Christmas. More boxes had been emptied, the items inside having found a place in the house or been given to charity. With fewer boxes, there was more room for the blow-up bed and a small dresser. Tony wouldn't have to live out of a suitcase for two weeks. Although she doubted it would matter to him. Men didn't seem to care as much about such things.

The pantry off the kitchen was well stocked, thanks to a recent visit to Costco in Boise. The freezer had plenty of meat, and the refrigerator had lots of summer fruits and vegetables. Since she still didn't know their exact plans for the next two weeks, it hadn't been easy to meal plan, but she'd done the best she could.

On Saturday morning she awakened with the knowledge that she would see Meredith in a matter of hours. Her stomach fluttered with excitement, and she was tempted to dress and drive down to the valley rather than leave it to Tony to meet Meredith at the airport and bring her to Kings Meadow. Of course it made sense for Allison to save herself the trip. Still, she knew the hours would crawl until she saw Tony's vehicle pull into the driveway.

She pushed herself up against the pillows and headboard. Her gaze went to the corner where Aunt Emma's old dressform now stood, wearing the wedding gown from the trunk. She'd brought them down from the attic a few weeks ago. Perhaps it was silly, but the dress—like the journals—made her feel close to her aunt. As if Aunt Emma were looking out for Allison and offering advice, one woman to another. There had been more to Emma Carter than met the eye. Much more. What Allison wouldn't give for the ability to sit down with her great-aunt and ask questions.

And her grandmother too. Grandma Elizabeth had died at a much younger age than her sister. Passed away in her sleep a few days after her great-granddaughter, Meredith Kavanagh, was born. Allison had been twenty-three, still young enough to believe life would go on unchanged forever. Not expecting a beloved grandmother could die unexpectedly. Now, all these years later, it seemed she'd hardly known Grandma Elizabeth at all.

Allison closed her eyes and pictured the sisters together. She supposed the women in her present memory had been in their seventies. Grandma Elizabeth had been a widow for at least a decade by then, and she often came to stay with her sister in her mountain home.

Laughter rang in Allison's head as she reminisced, and the sound made her smile. How those two loved to laugh. And argue! One of them would mention something about their childhood or their parents or some friend, and the other would state that the other's recollection was wrong. Then off they would go, each convinced her version of the story was the correct one.

Tony, whose own family was fractured and distant, had told Allison how fortunate she was, to have those two gems for grandmother and great-aunt. She'd agreed with him, but at the time, she hadn't known how true it was. Gizmo jumped onto the bed, causing Allison to open her eyes again. He whimpered once. Then his ears perked up and he lifted one paw, as if to shake her hand. The meaning was clear enough. Time to stop reminiscing, get out of bed, and get on with her day.

Emma

1932

"What do you think, Em? Would you like to live here?"

Emma turned from looking at the log house to facing her sister. "I couldn't possibly. It is too much for you and John to do. You've done so much already."

"We have never used it." Liza shifted the baby from the crook of her arm to her shoulder and patted him on the back. "John acquired it for almost nothing. He thought we could come for a few weeks in the summer. But it takes so long to drive up and with the children this small . . ." She fell silent, ending her words with a shrug.

Emma looked at the house again. A place to live far away from the reminders that haunted her in the valley. It was inviting. "I would insist on paying John back. I don't know when or how, but I couldn't let him give it to me outright."

Just *how* she would pay him back was a good question. And wouldn't it be even more difficult to earn some kind of income, living in these mountains? Yet her heart tugged at her to accept, even before she'd seen the interior of the two-story cabin. Somehow she knew the depression and fear that had gripped her since the divorce would not follow her to this log house. Somehow she knew this was where she would find peace at last. If God provided for her in this way, how could she refuse?

As if she sensed her sister weakening, Liza said, "Come with me. We'll look inside. Mark Thomas, come hold Aunt Emma's hand."

Emma's nephew darted over from the underbrush where he'd seen a chipmunk disappear. He held up his chubby little hand to her, and she took it, smiling. She seldom smiled these days, but her three-year-old nephew and his baby brother never failed to work their charms on her.

Liza led the way up the steep steps to the deck. She took a key from the pocket of her dress and unlocked the door. The interior of the house was dark and cool. While Liza went to open the drapes on the large front window, Emma moved into the center of the parlor. With a *whoosh*, the drapes were drawn to the sides and daylight spilled into the room, illuminating dust motes in the air.

"As you can see," Liza said, "we haven't bothered to furnish it. But we have everything you would need to set up house. John says you'll need an automobile to get into Kings Meadow but—"

"No. I couldn't accept a car in addition to the house. A horse and buggy would be sufficient."

"Em, really. You—"

"A horse and buggy. Or maybe a wagon would be more practical."

She walked into the kitchen. A large range took up most of the space on one of the outside walls. An icebox sat opposite it. A work table was in the middle of the room, and a sink with pump handle was located beneath the window. Anticipation stirred in her chest.

"No one in Kings Meadow would know you," Liza said from behind her. "They needn't know you're divorced or anything about Alexander. You could truly start over."

No one would know she'd ever been Mrs. Monroe. That was

what her sister meant. Erase the past. Just like ripping a wedding photo into a hundred pieces.

"The only drawback is that you will be so far away from the rest of the family. Well, that and the lack of electricity and indoor plumbing."

"Electricity is overrated. I wouldn't mind being without it."

"I would mind. I've grown spoiled by modern conveniences."

Emma left the kitchen and walked down the short hallway to the bedroom. It was roomy. Perhaps too large for a single woman.

"At least we wouldn't have to worry about Alexander's bootlegging friends looking for you here."

She turned to look at her sister. "That was months ago."

"Not long enough to suit me. Who knows what trouble Alexander will get himself mixed up in next?"

Emma had wondered the same thing for months. Not as often these days, but sometimes.

Liza walked to the bedroom window and looked out at the forest beyond the glass. "I'm not sure why, but I think this house would suit you."

It *did* suit her. Like shoes that were the right size or a pair of gloves. Here was where she was meant to be. Here she could find herself again.

"Tell John I accept."

Allison

A swirl of dust rose behind Tony's Ford truck as it came up the driveway. Allison watched from the deck, whispering a prayer for the next two weeks to be good for them all. Then she waved and went down the steps to meet them.

Meredith got a hug the instant she was out of the vehicle. Her daughter looked trim, tan, and healthy. As if she'd been on vacation all summer long.

"I hope you're using sunscreen when you're out in that Texas sun," Allison said before kissing Meredith's cheek.

"Always, Mom. You taught me well." She looked toward the ground. "Hey, Gizmo. How are you, guy?" She ruffled the dog's ears.

Allison turned to greet Tony across the hood of his truck. He looked good as well. "You're tanned too."

"I've started running again. Sunscreen in use." Grinning, he held up his hands, as if under arrest. "I promise." The smile faded a little. "Thanks for letting me come, Allie. I appreciate it."

As he spoke she realized she didn't mind his coming. Another layer of grief and anger had peeled away in the months since she'd seen him last.

"Come on." She looked back at her daughter. "Let's get the two of you settled in. It's been so hot the past couple of weeks. It's much cooler inside the house."

"Dad brought a bunch of camping stuff and our bikes,"

Meredith said. "I'm glad I left mine at the house instead of taking it to Texas. Are we still going up to Redfish Lake?"

"Of course, if you want to. This is your vacation. I'm just along for the ride."

Meredith hugged Allison. "You're the best," she whispered in her ear. "The absolute best."

Tony grabbed a suitcase and duffel bag from the bed of the truck. "I checked on availability. The week after Labor Day we shouldn't have any trouble getting a campsite. Not with schools back in session."

"Sounds like a good plan. The weather is supposed to stay warm and dry." Allison took the carry-on case from Meredith, then led the way into the house. "Same rooms as last time," she said when both of her guests were through the front door. "I'll get some iced tea ready while you put your things in your rooms."

Meredith and her father started up the stairs and Allison went into the kitchen. She'd made a large container of tea yesterday. Now she pulled the pitcher from the refrigerator, put ice in three glasses, and poured the beverage into them. Then she added a lemon wedge to the rim of each glass.

Voices carried to her from upstairs. Joyful voices punctuated with laughter.

Allison smiled. She'd learned to be content living alone. More than content. Comfortable. Happy, even. But all the same, it was good to have family in the house again. It was good to hear others laughing.

A few minutes later Meredith and her dad joined Allison in the kitchen. They stood, leaning against the counter and the island, sipping their tea while Meredith told them about the interesting gentleman she'd sat next to on the plane from San Antonio to Salt Lake City. He and his wife had adopted ten children from the foster care system. Meredith had pelted him with questions and been rewarded with stories that were heart-breaking, poignant, and amusing. "When the time comes," she concluded, "I'm going to adopt."

"Better wait until you have a husband," Tony said. "Anybody in mind?"

Meredith rolled her eyes. "I get so tired of that question."

Allison smiled at her without comment.

Then Meredith surprised her. "Actually, I *have* met someone special."

"What? When? You didn't say a thing when we talked last. Where did you meet him?"

Her daughter blushed, her expression one of pure pleasure. "His name is Rod. Rod Miller. We met at the humane society. We were both looking at dogs and we liked the same yellow lab mix puppy."

"You got a dog?"

"No. Rod got the dog. I was just looking and daydreaming. No place for a dog yet, especially not a puppy who's going to get so big. But he's the cutest thing. Big brown eyes. He's so fat he rolls off to one side when he sits."

Tony teased, "Rod's fat?"

"No!" Meredith gently punched her dad on the upper arm, both of them laughing. "The puppy's fat."

"I want to hear more about Rod," Allison said, trying not to sound *too* interested. In truth, the waiting was about to kill her.

"Okay." Meredith grinned. "He *does* have big brown eyes, but he's lean and tall. Not an ounce of fat on him anywhere. He's a Texan, through and through. Owns a couple of horses. Wears jeans and a cowboy hat most of the time. Works in support for a web-hosting company. Turns out he goes to the same church I do, but it's big and has several morning services so our paths never crossed."

Allison took a sip of her tea. "How long have you been dating?"

"Not long. Just a couple of weeks. But he's special, Mom. You know how you know about somebody, right from the start?"

"Yes. I know." She smiled softly. It had been like that for her and Tony. Her heart had known from the beginning. It hadn't taken long for her head to catch up.

Meredith drained the last of her iced tea. "Would anybody like to take a walk? I need some exercise after sitting all day on the plane and then driving up here."

Tony said, "Why don't you girls go without me? I'm sure there's some catching up you'd like to do."

His thoughtfulness caught Allison by surprise. *Thank you*, she mouthed to him. He nodded, then shrugged, as if to say, *No big deal.* But it was a big deal to her because thoughtfulness hadn't been his strong suit during their marriage.

When Allison and Meredith left, Gizmo on his leash, Tony followed them onto the deck where he settled into one of the chairs in the shade. "I'll be right here when you get back." Then he leaned back and closed his eyes, a smile on his face.

They walked down the drive and across the highway, then down the slope to the river.

Meredith stopped and stared at the rushing water. "I loved it up here over Christmas and New Year with all the snow, but this is even more beautiful."

"It *is* beautiful in the summer. I've taken lots of photos this year. I even bought myself a better camera and a couple of books on photography. Who knows? Maybe I'll become as good as Aunt Emma."

They resumed walking.

"Speaking of Aunt Emma," Allison said, "I made another find in the attic. She wrote a book about nature photography."

"Aunt Emma was published?"

Allison shook her head. "No. It's a manuscript. I don't know for certain when she wrote it or why it wasn't published. Maybe she tried and couldn't sell it, but that seems unlikely. She was highly regarded as a nature photographer. Never as famous as Ansel Adams, of course, but well-known enough that the public would have been interested in her book. I'm sure of it."

"Maybe you should try to get it published."

"I've thought of that. Susan thinks I ought to write a book about Aunt Emma, using pages from her journals and some of her photographs."

"Wow. That's a good idea too."

"Perhaps I could combine them. It would be kind of fun to honor Aunt Emma that way." Allison slipped her arm through Meredith's. "Now, tell me more about this Rod Miller fellow."

Emma

July 2, 1932

Tonight is my first night in my new home. Emma Carter, property owner.

The dark cloud I lived under these past months has lifted. Perhaps because I have been busy preparing for this move to the mountains near the town of Kings Meadow. Or perhaps it is because months have passed without seeing or hearing from Alexander, and not seeing him has helped ease the pain and the great sense of loss. Or maybe God took away the shadows so I might see the road ahead and begin following Him again.

When I think of Alexander, which I do often, I have learned to pray for him. I do not believe I did enough of that when he was my husband. If I had, perhaps our lives would have been different. While he was not the man I built him up to be in my mind and heart in the beginning, he is a man whom God loves and wants to redeem. So that is my prayer for him. That he will find God. That he will know peace.

After John and Father left this afternoon, I fed the horse the amount of hay I was told he needs. I've named him Copper because of his color. He's a big sturdy animal, over sixteen hands, and he looks quite handsome in harness. I took him out for a trot yesterday, and I found it delightful to drive a buggy again rather than an automobile. I believe that may well be my favorite thing about my new home.

After I fed Copper I prepared my own supper. The kitchen range is a marvel, I must say. It has six holes, a high shelf, and a low closet. It burns coal, which I much prefer for cooking. There is a man in Kings Meadow who will deliver both coal and ice, year-round, for a reasonable price. And while there are disadvantages to not having electricity and an indoor water closet, I do not believe I shall find it too egregious.

My parents are giving me an allowance to help me get by until I find a way to make some kind of living (whatever shall I do in that regard?). I did not want to accept, but they insisted and I had little choice. I am still dependent upon the kindnesses of my family, and they have been kind beyond my wildest dreams. I thought my divorce would be especially shameful to Mother, but if so, she has not let me know it.

Liza looked shocked when I suggested to her that I might learn to hunt so I can supplement my food stuffs, and I suppose it is a bit shocking for someone who was raised in town. I have never held a rifle in my life. But surely if I could climb trees and ride a horse bareback through the fields as a child, I could learn to shoot a rifle as an adult.

Allison

The first week of their vacation passed in a lazy August haze. They made no set plans, instead doing whatever struck their fancy at a moment's notice.

On Wednesday, they drove up to McCall and rented a boat to go around the lake. Allison loved looking at the old cabins she could see from the water. Many had been built early in the previous century. She loved to imagine the people who'd lived in them. There were lots of newer cabins too. Mansions, some of them, owned by the rich, some by the famous.

Tony got up in the cool of each morning and went for a run. He managed to return just in time for breakfast. Meredith teased him about it.

On Saturday they went into town to attend the Kings Meadow Annual Rodeo, an event held every Labor Day weekend. While it didn't rank up there with major rodeos like the Snake River Stampede, there were plenty of cowboys and cowgirls willing to travel to Kings Meadow, Idaho, to compete for the prizes. The rodeo had all of the usual events—bareback and saddle bronc riding, calf roping, steer wrestling, bull riding, barrel racing— and there were a couple unusual ones as well.

It was before noon when Chet Leonard sauntered along the bottom of the stands, reaching the steps nearest where Allison was seated. He stopped, looked up, and waved, then climbed toward her. "Morning, Allison." His gaze shifted to Tony, whom he'd met at church the previous Sunday. He bent his hat brim. "Morning, Tony. Meredith. You two having a good time?"

Meredith answered, "We sure are. The last time I was at this rodeo, Aunt Emma was alive. I must've been in high school or maybe even junior high."

Chet nodded, then focused on Tony. "We're looking for another team member for the wild cow milking. You interested?"

Allison felt her eyes widen at the request. Tony wasn't a cowboy. Athletic, yes. But wild cow milking? She couldn't imagine it.

"What would I have to do?"

That shocked her even more, that he was even considering it.

Chet answered, "You'd be one of the muggers. A rider gets the cow roped, then the muggers try to hold it still however they can. Still enough for one of them to get milk into a bottle. Doesn't have to be a lot. A few drops even. It's harder than it sounds, but the spectators love it. Event's not until later this afternoon. Probably around three o'clock, the way things are running now."

"Do it, Dad!"

Tony looked at Meredith. "Really?"

"Yes. It'll be fun."

"Fun for you, you mean." He raised an eyebrow.

Meredith laughed. "Of course."

Tony turned his eyes toward Allison. "What do you think?"

The strangest feeling coiled inside of her. She couldn't have described it to save her soul. Almost as if she were seeing him for the first time. Seeing him and liking what she saw. "I think you should do it too."

"If a cow kicks out my teeth, one of you is paying for my dental work." Tony looked at Chet. "Okay. I'm in."

Chet tugged the brim of his hat a second time. "Great. I'll let you know the time and place to meet with the rest of the team." He gave Allison a parting smile before heading down the stairs.

She watched Chet go, wondering what on earth had possessed him to ask Tony, of all people, to participate.

Tony intruded on her thoughts. "Maybe we'd better get something to eat. If I lose my teeth, I want to do it with a full stomach."

"Can you believe Dad's doing this?" Meredith asked as she and Allison stared toward the far end of the arena.

Tony was there with two other men on the ground. Chet was on horseback. Someone had given Tony a bright red shirt to wear. The rest of the team wore the same color. Tony was the only team member without a cowboy hat and western boots, and it made him stand out from the others.

"No, I can't believe it."

The Tony she'd known in college, the Tony she'd fallen in love with, would have done this kind of thing in a heartbeat. He'd been competitive by nature. Not so much the Tony of recent memories.

Out of the bucking chute came a solid black range cow. The animal's eyes were wide and frightened. Snot flew from its nostrils when it shook its head.

"Look at those horns," Meredith said.

Allison was looking. The cow looked as if it could do real damage with them. Her gaze darted to the end of the arena again in time to see Chet spur his horse into action, galloping toward the cow, rope swinging over his head.

Meredith shot to her feet as the rope sailed forward and over the cow's neck. "He's got her!"

The three muggers on the ground raced to the cow. One grabbed it by the horns, twisting its head. Another got it by the tail. Somehow Tony had ended up with the bottle. Had the men thought the rookie would have an easier time milking the cow than holding it still?

"Come on, Dad!"

"You can do it, Tony!"

As if he'd heard them, he glanced in their direction. Not more than a second or two—the event was timed and the clock was ticking—but long enough for Allison to see his grin. He was enjoying this. A lot.

The cow bellowed and fought. The muggers in front and behind were pulled this way and that. Chet tried to help by keeping the rope taut. Tony went for an udder. The cow twisted toward him, knocking him off his feet.

Allison and Meredith continued to scream words of encouragement, but their voices became part of the cacophony of the crowd. Everyone was shouting now. All the spectators were on their feet.

Tony was up again, attempting to grab an udder for the second time. The cow twisted and kicked and bucked and hopped. With his hatless head close to the cow's left back leg, his hands under her belly, Tony somehow stayed with the cow for a few seconds. Then he was knocked onto his backside a second time. But he held the bottle above him, as if protecting something of great worth.

The shouts of the crowd grew louder as he scrambled to his feet and raced toward the judge.

"He did it, Mom! He did it! Yea, Dad!"

Tony didn't lose any teeth in the wild cow milking, but he did return to the house wearing what looked like half the dirt from the arena, along with a small trophy for being on the winning team. Allison's stomach hurt from laughing so much and her throat was raw from the yelling she'd done from the stands.

"Ladies," Tony said as they entered the house, "I'm headed for the shower. If I'm not out of the bathroom in an hour, come rescue me. It means all this dirt I'm toting turned to mud and I'm stuck in it."

Feeling gritty herself, Allison went to her own bathroom to wash it away. By the time she finished showering and returned to the living room, Tony was downstairs and Meredith was taking her turn in the upstairs bathroom.

"Are you hungry?" Allison flopped onto the sofa.

"Too tired to be hungry," he answered from a nearby chair.

"Me too."

"I've got to admit. That's the most fun I've had in a long time. Crazy, but still fun."

Allison smiled. "You looked good out there." She closed her eyes, wondering if she might fall asleep mid-sentence.

"Allie?"

"Hmm."

"You saved my life."

She opened her eyes again.

"I know you think your tough love failed to do what it was supposed to, since I kept on drinking and we ended up divorced. But it didn't fail. If you hadn't stuck to your guns, if I hadn't been forced out on my own, I don't think I would have made it to this year."

"Tony," she said softly.

"So thanks. That's all. Just thanks."

She felt dangerously close to tears.

"Hey, Mom."

Allison straightened and looked toward the top of the stairs where Meredith stood, wrapped in a bathrobe, a towel on her head. "What, honey?"

"My blow dryer stopped working. Got one I can borrow?"

"Sure." Allison rose from the sofa, glad for a reason to leave the room so she could get her emotions in check. "I'll bring it right up."

"Thanks."

Allison hurried from the living room, through her bedroom, and into the master bathroom. She paused and leaned the heels of her hands on the counter while staring at her reflection. Her cheeks were flushed. From a day spent in the sun at the rodeo grounds or from something else? She didn't know. She felt off balance. Tony's words of thanks shouldn't have affected her so profoundly, but they did. She didn't care to look closer to discover the reason why.

Allison

September in Idaho was a glorious time of year, and no place was more so, in Allison's opinion, than the Stanley Basin.

They set up two tents—one for Allison, Meredith, and Gizmo; one for Tony—in a small campground overlooking Redfish Lake at the base of the Sawtooth Mountain Range. At sixty-five hundred feet above sea level, the nights were cold so they'd brought plenty of warm clothes. But it was pleasant enough in the daytime to need nothing more than a light sweater or a flannel shirt.

As soon as their camp was ready, they got on their bikes, Gizmo riding in the basket behind Allison's seat, and set off on a gently rolling trail that, the ranger told them, was six miles long, round trip, and had no more than a few hundred feet of change in elevation. It sounded like the perfect kind of ride for their first afternoon. And it was. They all had cameras, and no one seemed to mind when one of them wanted to stop to snap a photograph of a uniquely shaped tree or the sunshine shimmering on the surface of the lake or the rugged mountain peaks rising above them or a chipmunk scolding from a tree branch or a deer crossing the path ahead of them. But all those stops meant it took them better than an hour to complete the six-mile trail.

Once back at their campsite, Tony built a fire in the pit and Allison and Meredith got a start on dinner—grilled hamburgers on buns with all the fixings and homemade potato salad.

The threesome sat in low chairs around the campfire while

they ate. Gizmo tucked himself under Allison's chair and slept. No one talked much, except to say how good the food was. What was it about camping that made everything taste better than at home?

After swallowing her last bite of potato salad, Meredith said, "I've missed this."

"Me too," her dad answered.

Allison looked at Tony. Firelight flickered on his face as dusk settled around them. His voice echoed in her mind: *"I know you think your tough love failed to do what it was supposed to, since I kept on drinking and we ended up divorced. But it didn't fail."* A year ago she'd been angry at God for not saving her marriage. She'd been angry at Tony for not pulling himself up by his bootstraps and putting things right, angry because her dreams hadn't all come true. But it appeared God had been focused on saving Tony's life first. Saving it and then changing it.

Thank You, God. I'm glad Tony didn't die. I'm glad You saved him, both body and soul, even if it took ending our marriage to do it. I have a new life too, but I'm thankful he and I can be friends. You did that, Lord. You made it possible. Thank You for drawing Meredith and her dad close again. I'm glad she can be with and love her father. He's different now, yet he's still Tony. That's got to be Your doing, Lord.

The man of her prayers turned his head to look in her direction. "It's cooling off fast. Want your coat?"

Allison nodded.

"Me too, Dad."

He stood. "Be right back."

Meredith yawned. "I'll be turning in early. This alpine air is making me sleepy."

"How about s'mores before you go to bed?"

"You bet." Meredith sat up straight, looking alert again. "I'm always up for s'mores."

Allison laughed, pleasant memories washing over her of camping trips when their daughter was little. Of course, some of those trips had been spoiled by Tony's drinking, but the unpleasantness of *those* memories seemed to have faded.

"Here you go." Tony stood between Allison and Meredith, holding a coat in each hand.

Allison took hers and slipped her arms into the sleeves, thankful for the added layer as the evening temperature dipped. Then she pushed up from her chair. "We're going to make s'mores."

From the wooden box where they kept the food that didn't need a cooler—a sturdy container even small forest creatures couldn't gnaw through—she withdrew a box of graham crackers, a package of marshmallows, and a Giant Hershey's Milk Chocolate bar. Three wire hangers had been straightened into roasting utensils. She grabbed them too, along with paper plates.

Soon each of them was warming a marshmallow over the fire. Per tradition, everyone's goal was to get their marshmallow a golden brown on all sides. Conversation ceased as they concentrated on creating a *perfect* roasted marshmallow.

"Look out, Dad. Yours is about to drop."

Tony didn't heed the warning in time. As he tried to bring the wire upright, his marshmallow fell into the fire.

Meredith held her right hand to her forehead, making an L with her thumb and index finger, and her dad gave her arm a good-natured push. Then he took another marshmallow from the bag and started the roasting all over again.

Allison smiled to herself, treasuring the moment in her heart.

Emma

1932

The cat and her four kittens were in a blanket-lined crate in the back of the general store.

"What do you think, Miss Carter?" the proprietor asked. "Can we talk you into taking one of them home?"

Emma picked up the orange-colored tabby and brought it close to her cheek. "Aren't you precious?"

"Make a good mouser. Always good to have a cat to keep down the rodent population around a place. 'Specially the barn."

Emma glanced over her shoulder at Mr. Johnson. "Are they old enough to leave their mother?"

"Yep. They're eatin' and drinkin' on their own."

Emma reached down and grabbed the gray tabby with her other hand. "Then I'll take these two."

"Two of 'em, eh?" The store owner grinned. "The missus will be right pleased when I tell her they've gone to stay with you, Miss Carter."

It hadn't been difficult for him to convince her. After three months in her new home, Emma was ready for company, to hear some sounds she didn't make herself. She wasn't lonely. Not really. She had found her solitary existence to be good for her relationship with the Lord. She talked aloud to Him often. She wrote prayers in her journal. She'd learned to be still and know that He was God. But a couple of kittens would enliven her household and that appealed to her.

Mr. Johnson put the two kittens in an empty hatbox for the ride home. "Don't want 'em falling out of the buggy. Now, do we?"

Emma smiled at him as she took hold of the precious cargo.

With her grocery purchases in the back of the vehicle and the hatbox on the seat beside her, the kittens meowing noisily, Emma turned Copper toward home. October had painted the forest with rich golds and fiery reds, mixed in among the different shades of green. It wouldn't be long, she was certain, before the first snows fell. Her trips to town would be limited once winter set in. It could be six months or more before she was able to attend church services again. She would miss that more than anything.

She glanced down at the hatbox, then held the reins in her left hand and lifted the lid with the other. The two kittens looked at her with their round kitten eyes, still voicing their complaints.

"What shall I name you?"

"Meow. Meow."

"I know." She touched the head of the gray tabby. "You're Isaiah." She touched the gold-colored kitten. "And you're Jeremiah." She laughed as her gaze swept the surrounding forest and mountains. "Voices, crying in the wilderness." She slapped the reins against the horse's backside. "Giddy up there, Copper. Time we were home."

Copper's stride lengthened into a ground-eating trot and the buggy flew along the dirt road, leaving a cloud of dust in its wake. The kittens continued to yowl as Emma made a list in her head of things she needed to accomplish before nightfall. So intent were her thoughts she almost failed to slow the horse in time to turn into her driveway. And when she did, she was surprised to see her brother-in-law's automobile parked close to the house. She hadn't expected callers today.

Liza rose from a bench on the deck.

"Hello," Emma called to her, waving.

Liza waved back, bracing Harry, already six months old, on her left hip. "I was afraid I would have to leave before you returned."

Emma reined in. When the buggy stopped, she got down and tied the horse to a post, then grabbed the hatbox and hurried up the stairs. "How are you?" She kissed her sister's cheek.

"Fine. Everyone at home is well. Mother and Father too. I decided on a whim I wanted to see you before the weather turns, so here I am."

"I was thinking on the way home that it could snow soon." Emma kissed the top of Harry's head, his hair still little more than peach fuzz. "Where's Mark Thomas?"

"With his grandmother for the day."

"Oh. I'm sorry not to see him too. Come on inside."

"Are those kittens I hear in that box?"

Emma nodded as she opened the door.

"I hope they won't carry on like that for long."

"They won't. They're just scared. First time away from their mother."

Emma and Liza sat on chairs in the front parlor, and Emma put the hatbox on the floor, removing the lid as she straightened.

"Come on out, you two." She tipped the box slightly to make their escape easier. "Aren't they precious?" She ran her index finger over Jeremiah's back as his front paws touched the floor.

"Adorable. Are you going to put them in the shed with your horse and cow?"

"Heavens no! They'll stay in the house with me." Emma

held out her arms toward her sister. "Now, let me hold this chubby angel."

Liza passed the baby to her. "I brought you something. It's still in the car. I'll be right back." She rose and went out the front door.

While she waited for her sister's return, Emma kissed and nuzzled the baby in her arms until he giggled. Harry smelled good and his skin was soft. She ignored the small ache in her heart, that reminder of the babies she would never have, the memory of the one she'd lost. God had blessed her in many ways. What right did she have to complain about the things she didn't have?

The door opened, admitting Liza a second time. "I could have kept this for a Christmas present, but I didn't want to wait." She sat on the chair again, took Harry from his aunt, then passed a wrapped box to Emma. "Go on. Open it."

"Liza, you shouldn't have. You've done too much for me already."

"Hush. You don't even know what it is yet. You might not like it."

Emma removed the wrapping paper and opened the box. Inside was a camera.

"It's a Leica. Made in Germany. I was told it is the very latest thing."

"But, Liza, why—"

"You have never been particularly talented with a paintbrush, you don't enjoy knitting or crochet or needlepoint, and although you love to scribble your thoughts in those diaries you keep, I don't believe you have any desire to become a professional writer. But I know how much you love living in these mountains. Each time I see you I think how much you belong here."

Emma smiled at her sister, loving that she understood her so well. "I *do* belong here."

"Anyway, I thought you would enjoy taking photographs of the things and places you love."

"I don't know anything about photography."

"Of course not. But you'll have all winter to learn. And maybe, if you get good enough, you could sell your photographs."

"Sell them?" She looked at the camera in her hand, wondering how hard it might be to master. More difficult than learning to drive? "Do you really think so?"

"Em, you were always trying new things when we were girls. You were eager to learn. You were courageous and adventurous."

"I was, wasn't I."

"Yes, you were. Of course you've been a bit unsure of yourself in recent years, but I know the real you is still there, hiding underneath. You are the sort of woman who could make a name for herself in a man's world. Just see if you aren't."

Allison

They ate and slept. They went fishing. They rode bikes and took long hikes. They ate and slept and ate some more. And then it was Saturday and time to return to Kings Meadow. Anticipating her daughter's departure that same day made Allison sad. Two weeks had flown by, as she'd known they would.

Everyone in the SUV must have felt the same thing, for the two-hour drive home was much quieter than their drive to the Stanley Basin had been four days earlier. Even Gizmo rarely raised his head to look out the window. Once they arrived at the house, they removed the bikes from the carrier on the back of the Subaru. Tony's bike went back in his truck bed, along with the tents, his sleeping bag, and the rest of the camping gear. Meredith decided to leave her bike in Allison's garage, to be ready for the next time she visited.

Far too quickly, everything that was going down to Boise was loaded into Tony's truck, and there was nothing left to do but say good-bye.

"I love you, Mom." Tears strained Meredith's voice as she hugged Allison.

Don't cry, Meredith. If you cry, I don't stand a chance of holding it together.

"Make plans to come down to Texas for a visit this winter," her daughter added when the embrace ended.

"I will. For sure. Could you stand to have me for a week or so over Christmas?"

"You know I could. I could stand you anytime and for as long as you want to stay."

"Maybe I could meet Rod when I come."

Meredith shrugged. "Maybe." Then she smiled. "I hope so, anyway."

Allison swallowed the lump in her throat and turned toward Tony. "It was good seeing you."

"You too, Allie. Went by too fast."

"Yes, it did."

He walked up close and gave her a light hug. A tentative one, as if he was uncertain she would welcome it. "I like Chet Leonard, by the way. Seems like a good guy." He took a step back.

"Chet? What do you m—" Except she knew what Tony meant.

"If it wasn't for Chet, I wouldn't have that cool trophy to show all my friends when I get home." He winked before returning to the driver's side of the cab.

Allison watched as the two of them got into Tony's pickup. She waved as the truck headed down the driveway, not stopping until it disappeared from view. With her houseguests gone, the silence of the forest seemed absolute, and she couldn't hold back the tears any longer. Gizmo seemed to understand his mistress's distress. He pawed her leg and whimpered. She picked him up, burying her face in his coat.

"I hate the end of vacation."

Gizmo twisted around and licked her temple.

She smiled sadly as she set him on the ground. "We'd better get started on the laundry."

The dog ran ahead of her, up the steps to the deck, then looked back as he waited by the front door.

Stepping through the doorway, Allison stopped, letting her gaze travel around the living room and up the stairs. The silence had followed her inside. She crossed to her stereo system and turned on her iPod. She selected a playlist of favorite movie soundtracks and turned the volume up higher than normal, hoping to sing the blues away.

In the bedroom, serenaded by Carly Simon, Allison unloaded her suitcase, piling dirty clothes on the floor at the foot of the bed. Then she carried a load's worth to the laundry room and shoved the clothes into the front-loading washer. She filled the dispenser with soap, punched a few buttons, and turned a knob, each one beeping at her.

With the washer started, she walked into the kitchen—Ella Fitzgerald sang to her now—and began unloading the cooler Tony had left on the floor next to the refrigerator. Ketchup. Mustard. Miracle Whip. Two hotdogs left in a plastic baggie. Half an onion. One can of Diet Coke. Two mini-bottles of Diet Dr. Pepper, one of them half-empty. Some leftover baked beans.

Despite those items, the refrigerator remained in a depleted state. Amazing how much food three people could go through in two weeks' time. She would need to go into Kings Meadow to do some grocery shopping if she wanted anything decent to eat in the days to come. But not today. After church tomorrow would be soon enough.

"She's Like the Wind" came on the player, a song that pulled her back to the eighties. To memories of college and Tony. To the golden future that had stretched before them when they married. If Tony hadn't—

She cut off the thought. It was understandable Meredith's departure had left her sad and a bit lonely, but she didn't want to fall back into wishing for what might have been. It wasn't helpful or healthy.

"I need to take a shower." She glanced down at her faithful companion. "And you, sir, need a bath too."

The telephone rang, and Allison's eyes went to the clock on the kitchen wall. Much too soon for Meredith to be calling from the airport. Her flight didn't leave Boise until five thirty. She and her dad would stop to eat before he dropped her at the airport.

She picked up the handset from its cradle, not looking at the Caller ID. "Hello."

"Hey there." Susan. "How was the camping trip?"

"Good. Too short. We had a great time and couldn't have asked for better weather. We were the only people in the campground the whole time we were there, but another family was checking in this morning while we were breaking camp."

Susan said something, but Allison couldn't understand her.

"Hold on a second. I've got the music on too loud." She hurried into the living room and turned down the sound. "What did you ask?"

"Have Tony and Meredith left?"

"Yes. Maybe half an hour or forty-five minutes ago."

"How're you doing?"

There came that doggone lump in her throat. She swallowed it. "Okay."

"Really?"

"No. I'm missing Meredith."

Susan was silent for a few heartbeats before asking, "And Tony?"

"What about him?"

"Are you missing him too?"

"No . . . Maybe . . . I don't know."

Susan laughed. "Maybe you need to figure out which of those it is."

"Susan, haven't we been over this before? If you're suggesting I might want to get back together with Tony, you are *way* off the mark. That ship sailed a long time ago. Sure, I care about him. You and I've talked about that before too. He's the father of my daughter. I'm glad we can be friends. But I wouldn't want to go down that same road again. Not for anything. I let go, the way God told me to. Now I'm moving on."

"Are you trying to convince me or yourself?"

"Neither," she answered, more sharply than she meant to. "Just speaking the truth."

"Okay. Okay. I didn't mean to make you mad."

Allison drew a deep breath and let it out. "I'm not mad." And she wasn't. She just didn't want her thoughts to go in that particular direction a second time today, with or without her friend's queries.

"I'm glad you're not mad. Now that that's settled, want to come for dinner after church tomorrow?"

"I'd better not. I've a lot to do after having fun the last two weeks. I need to catch up so I can hit the ground running on Monday."

With any luck, all that work she needed to do would get her over the hump of missing her daughter.

Allison

The Kings Meadow Community Theater performed *The Importance of Being Earnest* on the last weekend of September. Susan and Ned went with Chet and Allison to the Friday evening production. At the restaurant afterward, they unanimously declared the play wonderful and funny. Then each ordered a different kind of pie. When the dessert came, the plates were moved around the table clockwise, everybody getting a taste of each confection.

Music played softly through the truck's speakers as Chet drove Allison home. They seemed to have run out of conversation, riding in silence along the ink-dark highway. Only when Chet turned his pickup into Allison's driveway did he speak.

"I enjoyed tonight. Glad you weren't so busy you couldn't go."

Allison had been too busy to do anything but work over the last three weeks. She'd begged off from several invitations—Chet's and others—before tonight. "I'm glad I could go too. It was fun."

Chet braked to a halt and killed the engine. The dash lights remained lit, bathing the interior of the cab in an eerie glow. Chet turned to face her. "There's something I need to tell you, and I didn't want to do it over the phone or in front of Susan and Ned. I'll tell them later."

A shiver of alarm passed through her. She wasn't ready for more of a commitment. If he was about to ask—

"I'm going down to Reno. To see Marsha."

Alarm was followed by relief.

"She's finally agreed to meet with me," he said.

Allison nodded, not sure what would be the right thing to say.

"She's been seeing a counselor this summer, and she wants to talk about what went wrong."

"I'm glad, Chet. It should be good for both of you. When are you going?"

"Next week." He cleared his throat. "I thought I was ready to let go of her, Allison, but I'm not. Even after the divorce I'm not. I want the boys to have their mother with them, if at all possible. And I'd like my wife to come back too, if and when she's ready."

"Of course that's what you want."

"I didn't mean to lead you on. I like you a lot, but I—"

"You didn't lead me on, Chet. I'm glad to have you for a friend. I'm not ready for more than that either. Others might not understand, but I do."

He was silent for a time, then said, "I'll walk you to the door." He got out of the cab.

Allison waited for him to come around and open her door. She also waited to feel at least a little disappointment. But she wasn't disappointed. Not in the least. It truly was enough for them to be friends and nothing more. The door opened and Chet offered his hand to help her down from the cab. Then they walked side by side up the steps to the front door.

After unlocking the door, Allison looked at Chet again. "I'll be praying for your meeting with Marsha."

"Thanks. I'll take all the prayer I can get."

"Good night, Chet."

"Night, Allison." He turned on his heel and returned to his pickup.

Gizmo greeted Allison with his usual excitement when she

entered the house. She told him to wait as she listened for the sounds of Chet's departure. Only after she knew he was gone did she take Gizmo outside.

The night was chilly, and she pulled her sweater more tightly about her as she waited for the dog. Overhead, the sky was clear and dotted with countless stars, some looking close enough for the treetops to touch. Her second winter in this house would soon be upon her.

Her thoughts went to Aunt Emma, as was common. Although Allison hadn't read about it yet in the diaries, she'd heard stories of her aunt's early days in the log house. No indoor plumbing other than a pump in the kitchen sink. No electricity, so lighting had come from oil lamps and candles. Heating had come from wood in the fireplace in the living room and coal in the range in the kitchen.

What a difference eighty years made.

Last winter Allison had paid to have a man keep her driveway plowed so she could still come and go in her SUV. What had Aunt Emma done? She must have been trapped in the house for months at a time some winters. How had she stood it? She'd already had so much to bear. A lonely marriage. A miscarriage. And apparently a cheating husband.

Last night Allison had read the entry where Aunt Emma wrote her suspicions about Alexander's infidelity. It was hard not to hate the louse, even decades later. But Aunt Emma hadn't hated him, at least not yet. Obviously Emma Carter had been a more forgiving person than Allison was. If Tony had ever been unfaithful—

"Pray for Tony, Allison."

She could see in her mind where Aunt Emma had stood when she said those words.

"Pray without ceasing. We are often ignorant of the work

God is doing in the unseen realms. Miracles happen when we least expect them."

"But I didn't get the miracle, Aunt Emma," she whispered now. "I prayed. I wanted it. But I didn't get it."

Emma

May 23, 1933

Spring is here at last. Copper and my milk cow are shedding their winter coats. The hens spend more time outside the coop than in it. And Isaiah and Jeremiah have discovered a whole new world out of doors. I worry they will get eaten by a predator, but they refuse to be shut up inside so I must let them have their freedom, despite the dangers.

Freedom. I thought much about the word over the winter. I contemplated what it means to be free in Christ, and I resolved that freedom in Christ is the only kind of freedom worth anything. Every other kind of freedom pales beside it. And if I am free in Christ, then I will know freedom wherever He leads me, even if He should lead me into a prison cell, as He did the apostle Paul, or into a solitary life in a log house in the mountains of Idaho, as it seems to be now for me.

I continue to pray for Alexander. I wish he might know this freedom too. I understand now, as I could not understand before, that he was bound up on the inside. I wanted him to fill my every need, needs that can only be filled by the King of Kings. It is not fair to put that kind of burden on another human being. I am sorry for putting that burden on Alexander. I wish I could tell him that.

Allison

Thanksgiving was just four weeks away. Christmas another four and a half weeks after that. Allison had made her arrangements for the trip to Texas, departing on the eighteenth of December. She would stay with Meredith over Christmas and New Year's and return to Idaho on the third of January.

But what to do about Thanksgiving? Last year she'd played hostess to her daughter and some of her new Kings Meadow friends. This year she'd received several invitations to the homes of others, but she had yet to accept any of them. What was her problem? Why did she feel trapped by inertia?

It was a Thursday morning. Allison sat at the kitchen table, her Bible open to the book of Galatians on the left, her journal open on the right. She wrote the final words of a prayer and, when the pen stopped moving, whispered, "Amen."

And that was when she heard His voice in her heart, as clear as if it were audible. *It would bring Me pleasure.*

She didn't have to ask God what would bring Him pleasure. It was mysterious, the way the Holy Spirit communed with the spirit of men and women who followed Him, but it was clear. He meant Tony. It would bring Him pleasure if she was with Tony.

For Thanksgiving?

For life.

She couldn't seem to draw breath.

It would bring Me pleasure.

Maybe hearing His voice wasn't as easy and clear as she'd thought. God wouldn't say *that* to her. It was the Lord Himself who'd told her to let go, to move on, to make a new life for herself. She'd obeyed. Surely God wouldn't ask her to go back.

What if this was a trick of the enemy?

Icy tentacles circled her heart.

Or worse, what if God *was* asking her to go back and Tony's sobriety didn't last?

It would bring Me pleasure.

She got up from the chair and left the kitchen. At the living room window, she stared outside. The gold of the tamaracks and aspens mixed with the green of the lodgepole and ponderosa pines. So beautiful. It was the home the Lord had provided. A place for her to retreat to, a place where she was able to heal. Would He truly ask her to leave it?

The phone rang. She was tempted to ignore it, but before it went to voice mail, she reached for the handset.

"Hey, Allie."

Her heart stopped and then raced. Why had Tony called at *this* exact moment? Right now when she felt confused and afraid.

"I thought maybe you weren't home."

"No. I'm here."

She hadn't talked to Tony in six or seven weeks, and yet he'd called her now. The timing seemed too exact to be coincidence.

"I heard you're definitely going down to Texas for Christmas."

"Yes."

"Well, I was wondering if you'd like to join me for Thanksgiving."

God, this is crazy. I have to be mistaken.

"A couple of guys from my recovery group and their wives are coming over. One of them's my sponsor. It wouldn't just be the two of us, if that's what you're wondering."

It wasn't.

"How about it?" he pressed.

She could tell him she had another invitation. It was the truth. She had several. He didn't have to know she hadn't accepted any of them yet.

"Allie?"

She let out a held breath. "Okay. I'll be there unless the roads are bad. What can I bring?"

"A couple of pies?"

"Sure. Pumpkin and cherry okay?"

"You bet. I'm glad you can come, Allie. I'll talk to you again before Thanksgiving gets here." He was silent a moment, then said, "If you want to bring somebody, it's all right with me."

He meant Chet. He believed she and Chet were an item. She'd let him believe it even though they weren't. Yet God had already removed any chance of there being another man in her life. Hadn't He? At least that was how it seemed in this moment.

To Tony, she said, "No. There's no one I want to bring. Unless you mean a little four-legged somebody. Have dog. Will travel."

Tony laughed. "Gizmo's always welcome."

The sound of his laughter seemed to quiet her unsettled spirit.

They said good-bye, and Allison punched Off on the handset.

"Lord, I hope You know what You're doing."

Allison

Early on Thanksgiving morning Allison lay in bed, nestled beneath her down comforter, reluctant to get up. She wasn't in any great hurry. She'd made the pies yesterday. The roads were clean and dry. Even with plans to arrive at Tony's house before the other guests, she didn't need to leave for several more hours.

She drew a deep breath and let it out slowly. When she opened her eyes, she turned her head on her pillow, her gaze going to the corner of the bedroom, to the dress form and wedding dress Emma had worn with a heart full of hope, not imagining the difficulties that lay ahead of her.

Allison had reached 1932 in Aunt Emma's diaries. Some of the entries had brought her to tears. She'd cried for her aunt and for herself too. Their situations were similar in many ways and yet dissimilar in others. Through the pages of these journals, Allison had not only unearthed a family secret, but she'd watched her great-aunt mature from an uncertain, unhappy, sometimes desperate wife into a strong woman of faith. Emma hadn't been born with faith and strong character. God had allowed life to mold her, to refine her.

Grandma Elizabeth, according to one entry, had told Aunt Emma divorce wasn't the unforgivable sin. But Allison knew from experience divorce often felt like it was, even when infidelity or abandonment by an unbelieving spouse gave a person biblical permission to end a marriage. Was that why Aunt Emma had gone to her grave keeping her failed marriage a secret? Or had it been only to please her sister? Perhaps future journals would tell her that.

Allison closed her eyes again and prayed for the day ahead. She prayed for a safe drive down to Boise and back again. And she asked God to make it clear what she should say to Tony today. *If* she should tell him what she'd felt God speak to her. Did she dare tell him? It wasn't as if Tony had said he wanted more than the congenial relationship they now enjoyed.

With a sigh, she tossed aside the bed coverings and sat up. She was tired of wrestling with the questions and confusion. She hoped a shower would wash them away for a few hours.

———

Since moving out of the house a year and a half before, Allison had not been near her old home, let alone inside of it. It felt strange to stand on the stoop and ring the doorbell.

Tony answered the ring, an oven mitt on one hand. He grinned. "You made it."

Her stomach fluttered as she set Gizmo down and watched the dog run into the house as if he remembered being there as a puppy.

"Come in," Tony said.

Allison drew a tentative breath and stepped inside, her gaze sweeping the living and dining rooms. It was both familiar and foreign. Tony hadn't bothered to replace the furniture she'd taken with her to Kings Meadow, so it felt empty. A woman's touch was definitely absent.

Tell him.

Her pulse quickened. She wasn't ready. She couldn't. She didn't know what to say. She would never know what to say. What if she said the wrong thing? What if—

"I'm about to mash the potatoes." Tony closed the door.

"Okay if I let you hang up your own coat? Join me in the kitchen when you're through." He held out his hands to take the tray holding the two pies.

She handed it to him, then removed her coat and hung it in the entry closet. When she entered the kitchen a few moments later, she said, "Smells good in here."

"Hopefully I haven't ruined the turkey and stuffing. First turkey I've ever been in charge of roasting." He turned off the burner under the pot of potatoes. "I was tempted to call you about six o'clock this morning to make sure I was doing it right."

"I'm glad you didn't call." Allison sat on one of the tall stools behind the island. "I slept in for a change."

Tony turned from the stove and shot her a smile. "It's good to have you here."

"It's good to be here." Fear tried to remind her of all that had gone wrong within these walls. Faith pushed the bad memories away.

"Want something to drink? I made coffee a little while ago, and there's diet soda in the fridge if you'd rather have something cold."

"I'm good for now. Thanks."

Gizmo pranced up and sat on the floor in front of Tony.

"Smell the turkey, buddy?" Tony said.

The dog lifted a paw, begging with his eyes.

"Sorry." Tony shook his head. "I know the rule. No people food for Gizmo's sensitive stomach." He looked at Allison. "Right?"

Tell him.

Her insides felt tied in a gazillion knots as she opened her mouth. That was when the doorbell rang. Gizmo darted out of the kitchen and Allison closed her mouth. Tony went to open the door.

While Tony welcomed his guests and took their coats, Allison got off the stool and made herself useful, draining water from the pot of boiled potatoes. She found a large mixing bowl where she'd kept them. The new hand mixer was stored in its proper place too.

Tony reappeared in the kitchen doorway, followed by two couples, both of the women carrying their contributions to the Thanksgiving meal. One of the couples looked familiar to Allison. The others were strangers. Tony performed quick introductions. Although he introduced her as Allison Kavanagh, he left off the fact that she was his *ex*-wife. She supposed they knew that.

Thanksgiving dinner was a pleasant affair. The conversation was enjoyable, and Allison felt among friends. She couldn't help noticing how comfortable Tony was as he played host. How at ease he made others feel too. It hadn't always been that way.

"I loved you, Allie. I did. Still do, though I know you don't want to hear it."

No, back in April she hadn't wanted to hear those words from Tony. Was she ready now? Had his feelings changed? Had hers?

God? Help!

Before she knew it, several hours had passed, and the other guests made their farewells. This time Allison went to the door with Tony. Almost as if . . .

"I'd better go too," she said.

"Do you have to?"

She nodded. "I prefer not to drive the river highway in the dark."

"Let me give you some of the leftovers."

"You don't have—"

"It'll go to waste if you don't take some. I think the bird was on the large size for a group of six."

Allison followed him back to the kitchen and watched as he filled disposable plastic containers with some of everything.

And then, unexpected and unbidden, the words tumbled from her mouth.

"Tony, do you think we could put this thing back together?"

What amazed her later, though not in the moment, was that he didn't have to ask what she meant by "this thing." He looked at her, tears welling in his eyes—he wasn't a man who cried easily or often but he was on the verge of doing so now—and nodded. "Yes," he said, almost too softly to hear. "Yes, I believe we can."

"I think that's what God wants," she rushed on. "But I'm not sure. It frightens me, Tony. We need to pray about it. Both of us. A lot. We need to seek wise counsel." She turned her back to him, trying to bring her emotions into check.

"Whatever you want, Allie."

Should she have said anything? Had this been the right time? What if she'd heard wrong? She'd heard wrong before. Her calm and contented little world could crumble around her ears if she was mistaken.

She faced Tony again. "I need to go." She couldn't keep the edge of panic from her voice.

After another nod, he put the containers of food into a canvas bag and held it out to her. She took it without another word and made her escape as fast as was possible.

Emma

August 3, 1933

Dear Liza,

I have sold three of my photographs to a magazine. Amazing! You believed in me when I could not believe in myself. I have learned a great deal about lighting and positioning and developing. Some days I do nothing but shoot and develop photographs. Housework and cooking seem unimportant when I am caught up in creative activity.

Photographing God's beautiful creation has become one of my greatest joys. Try though I might, I can never quite capture completely what I see, what I want to convey, which only makes me more eager to try again and again.

I received a letter last week from Mrs. Conners, the woman I used to work for. She wrote that she saw Alexander recently and he looks ill. I know you do not want me to ask about him, but he weighs heavy on my heart. No matter what he did in the past, I continue to ask God to draw him close and to bless him. Please, if you chance to see him, tell him I am praying for him. Tell him, if I knew where to send a letter, I would write to him.

I am sending you some of the photographs I took of Mark Thomas and Harry the last time we were together. They are the two most adorable boys ever. I seldom miss living in the city. I am happy in my mountain home. But I do miss being able to see my nephews more often. They change so fast between visits.

I send my love to you and John and the boys. Tell Mother I will write to her and Father soon.

Your sister,
Emma

Allison

It took Allison two days to work up the nerve to call her most trusted friend and mentor. And when Allison said she needed to talk, Susan didn't ask what it was about. She simply said she would come over without delay. While Allison waited, she paced the house like a caged panther in a zoo.

Should it bother her that Tony hadn't called yesterday or today? It did. Then again, it didn't. She wasn't sure. Her thoughts were a complete jumble.

Earlier in the year she had written in her journal that the best way to confirm God's will included three steps: knowing His character so as not to act against it; receiving reconfirmation; and asking for wise counsel from another Christian. Now she was trying to apply that lesson. Certainly God's character would approve of a reconciliation between husband and wife. And despite her churning thoughts and crazy emotions, she believed God had reconfirmed His will in a number of ways. Finally, she was about to ask for counsel from Susan Lyle.

When her friend arrived, they settled on chairs at the kitchen table, cups of coffee in their hands. Bless Susan's heart, she didn't push for more information. She waited until Allison was ready. When she was, the words poured out of her in a rush, beginning with the day she'd heard God's voice as she journaled right up through Thanksgiving Day when she'd asked Tony if he thought they could or should reconcile.

Allison stopped talking as suddenly as she'd begun.

Susan's smile was warm and gentle. "That is quite the development, isn't it?"

Not quite the wise counsel Allison had hoped for.

"Allison, we cannot trust our emotions to be our guides. Yours are all over the map right now."

"I know. But what do you think?"

"It doesn't matter what I think, really. Besides, you already know what God wants. Don't you?"

Allison drew a deep breath and closed her eyes. "But what if I heard wrong again? I was so sure God promised to save my marriage and look what hap—" She stopped, stunned by the realization that swept over her. Then she started to cry. Not dainty tears but noisy, ugly sobs.

Susan got up and came to sit beside her, drawing her close until the tears were spent and she quieted again.

Finally, Allison lifted her head from Susan's shoulder. "I will never forget the day when I was so sure God promised to save my marriage. I thought the promise meant things would get better from that moment on. But Tony walked out and his drinking got worse and worse. So bad I thought he would die. God told me to let go of him. I thought that was the end, that it was proof God hadn't promised to save my marriage, that I must have misunderstood Him. But maybe I didn't misunderstand. Maybe He *is* saving my marriage. Maybe He saved it by ending it first."

Susan smiled. "What an unexpected way to keep a promise."

Emma

1933

The envelope held a clipping from the newspaper and a letter. Emma looked at the clipping first and felt her heart skip a beat. It was the obituary of Alexander James Monroe, who'd passed away on October 1 at the age of twenty-nine. Little other information was included. Only that he'd been preceded in death by his parents and had lived his whole life in Boise City.

Sinking onto a chair, Emma unfolded the letter. She recognized Alexander's handwriting at once, though it seemed unsteady on the page.

September 20, 1933

Emma,

I asked a friend to mail this letter after I am gone. If you are reading it, then I am dead. Should not be long now. The doctors say my liver and kidneys are failing, and I will not recover. The best I can hope for is to go quickly. I am not strong enough to write all I would like to but I will say what I can.

I am sorry for hurting you. More sorry than words can express. I was cruel to you and I had no reason to be. You loved me and cared for me, even at my worst. The hurt I caused cannot be undone, but I hope *you will forgive me. Liza—when she told me how to reach you, though I could tell she did not want to do so—told me you forgave me long ago.*

You may not believe this, Emma, but I am a changed man. But like the thief on the cross, it is too late for me to prove I am different to anyone. The blood of Christ has made me so. All those times someone tried to share that truth with me, and I would not listen. How I regret it now.

I know you prayed for me while we were married, and I suspect you kept on praying for me even after we were divorced. I want you to know your prayers bore fruit. Jesus saved me from my sins, and heaven will be my home, undeserving though I am.

Alexander James Monroe

A tear dropped from Emma's cheek onto the letter, blurring the ink of his signature. Her heart ached, but mostly her tears were tears of joy. God had answered her prayers for Alexander, and whatever the future held for her, she would remember His faithfulness to her. She would remember the grace He had poured out on Alexander.

For all of the promises of God were yes and amen in Christ Jesus her Lord.

It was a truth Emma knew would carry her through the rest of her life. No matter how many or how few years that might be.

Allison

Tony and Allison Kavanagh were remarried on Valentine's Day, in a brief but intimate ceremony, surrounded by close friends and loved ones. Allison wore Aunt Emma's wedding dress. "It deserves a happy ending," she'd told Meredith, not caring if it sounded idiotic. And since the dress fit Allison as if it were made for her, that seemed to confirm her decision.

When counseling with the pastor before the wedding, she and Tony decided they didn't want to repeat individual vows to each other. They wanted to speak the same words at the same time. They would use words from a favorite psalm, one that had taken on new meaning in the weeks leading up to the wedding.

When the time came in the ceremony, they turned, looked into each other's eyes, took hold of each other's hands, and said, "This is the Lord's doing. It is marvelous in our eyes. This is the day which the Lord has made. Let us rejoice and be glad in it. Give thanks to the Lord, for He is good. For His lovingkindness is everlasting."

And He keeps His promises in unexpected ways.

"Amen."

A Note to Readers

Dear Friends:

A Promise Kept is a special story to me because I have walked a similar path to the one Allison walked. I wrote this book, in part, as my thanks to God for holding me close in the valleys and for answering prayers in unexpected ways.

While I am not Allison and she is not me, I was married to an active alcoholic, Jerry, who was in and out of rehab, who was prayed for countless times by friends, elders, and pastors, and whom I loved with all of my heart. Because of our particular journey, I learned what it means to be refined and to thank God in all circumstances. I would not be the woman I am or the believer I am were it not for the circumstances of my life, including my marriage. But because I was convinced God had promised to save my marriage several years earlier, I believed Jerry would get better.

Only, things didn't happen the way I'd envisioned. He got worse. After a year of separation when I hoped and prayed for reconciliation, God told me to let go and I found myself divorced. I was devastated. I sank into a period of deep mourning over the death of my marriage. It lasted for many months. Sometimes I thought the sorrow would be with me forever. Like Allison, I knew that God doesn't lie, which had to mean He hadn't promised to save my marriage. I'd misunderstood. Unlike Allison, I drew closer to the Lord and leaned into Him for support and comfort.

I suppose Jerry and I had an unusual relationship as exes. We still cared for each other. We sat together in church most Sundays. We went to see movies each Christmas since he had no family nearby. Occasionally, we took bike rides together. I saw him changing over the years and was glad for him. But I was content with my life and thought it would continue on as it was.

And then, almost five years after the divorce was final, I was at my desk, writing in my journal, and I felt God say that it would bring Him pleasure if Jerry and I were together. My first response was not to answer, "Yes, Lord." It was more along the lines of, "No way! God wouldn't ask that of me."

Every time I saw Jerry after that, I would feel a nudge to tell him about it, but I was afraid. I'd been wrong before when I believed God promised to save my marriage. What if I was wrong again? How could I take the chance?

Five or six weeks later, after a lovely evening bike ride along the Boise River (during which I'd felt those same nudges multiple times), Jerry was preparing to leave my house and I blurted out, "Do you think we could put this thing back together?"

We hadn't been talking about anything personal. Certainly not about marriage. There is no reason why he should have known what "this thing" even was. But he did know. He teared up and nodded. But I was already back-pedaling in fear of taking a misstep. I told him I would have to talk to my friends at our annual retreat (I was leaving for it soon after this). We would have to attend counseling. We would have to pray. We would have to move slowly. Maybe we shouldn't even think about it.

The women I gather with each summer in Northern Idaho are a very special group of friends. For over a decade now, we have prayed together and laughed together and loved on one another and wept copious tears when the hardships of life have hit one of us. I trust them with my deepest secrets and they trust me. Above everything, these women love the Lord and know His Word. They are godly women whose wise counsel I can depend on.

I was certain that when I told them what was going on (I waited until I was with them face-to-face), at least one of them would say, "Are you nuts?" But no one did. Instead, there were words of praise, and I felt the Spirit calm my fears in an instant.

And then it hit me. I hadn't heard wrong. God had promised to save my marriage. He was saving it through the rubble of divorce. Divorce had looked like a permanent failure to me, but God had used it for good in both of our lives.

Jerry and I were remarried two months later.

God answered my prayers for my marriage, not in the ways I expected or even wanted, certainly not in the timing I wanted, but in the ways and timing He chose. God can and does work miracles. He can instantly cure an illness or an addiction. But more often than not, Jesus invites us to be yoked with Him as we walk through the fire together. He matures us in the refining process so that we might become more like Him.

Psalm 118 has become a very special psalm to me. The pastor read it at our wedding. It represents in many ways the trials Jerry and I have walked through and the faithfulness of God in it all. I consider verses 23–24 and 29 to be the theme of our marriage today:

> This is the Lord's doing;
> It is marvelous in our eyes.
> This is the day which the Lord has made;
> Let us rejoice and be glad in it . . .
> Give thanks to the Lord, for He is good;
> For His lovingkindness is everlasting. (NASB)

My prayer for you, dear reader, is that your eyes may be open to all of the unexpected ways God is keeping His promises to you, now and in the years to come.

In the grip of His grace,
Robin Lee Hatcher
www.robinleehatcher.com

Reading Group Guide

1) Allison moved to a new place to begin her life anew. Have you ever done the same? How did you settle in and become part of your new setting?

2) Before Allison moved to Kings Meadow, she had drifted away from church and other believers because she felt like a failure. Have you ever allowed your faith to "drift"? How did you find your way back?

3) Alcoholism is sometimes called a "disease of secrets" because family members often hide what is happening in the home. Has your life been impacted by a loved one with addictions of any kind? If so, have you been able to reach out to someone to help you find healing and hope?

4) Emma thought that marriage would fill the need in her heart. Then she thought a child would fill that need. Have you looked for fulfillment in people or situations rather than in Christ? What were the end results?

5) Allison learns to accept her "new normal." Have you had to do the same? Can you share how God helped you with it?

6) Emma kept journals for decades, and Allison began following her example. Do you journal? If so, do you find that God speaks to you through this exercise?

7) God saves Allison and Tony's marriage by first allowing it to crumble. How has God answered prayers in your life in totally unexpected ways?

8) Tony and Allison used verses from Psalm 118 for their wedding vows. Are you able to look at sometimes difficult experiences in your own life and see that "this is the Lord's doing" and it is marvelous in your eyes?

Acknowledgments

Thanks first and foremost to my husband, Jerry, who has given me the freedom to use our lives as the inspiration for *A Promise Kept* (among other stories).

Thanks to Ami for the encouragement to write the story that was on my heart. You are a writer's delight!

Thanks to Natasha for being such a great partner in my crazy life as a novelist.

Thanks to the ladies who plot, play, and pray every summer in Coeur d'Alene: Brandilyn Collins, Francine Rivers, Gayle DeSalles, Janet Ulbright, Karen Ball, Mama Ruth, Sharon Dunn, Sunni Jeffers, Tamera Alexander, and Tricia Goyer. You have spoken faith and hope into my life for more than a decade, and I cannot imagine going through life without all of you in it. You didn't help brainstorm this particular book, but your handprints are all over it just the same.

With her world spinning out of control, Katherine
wonders if she can find the truth in the chaos
that consumes her. How can she survive the
loss of what she thought was the perfect life?

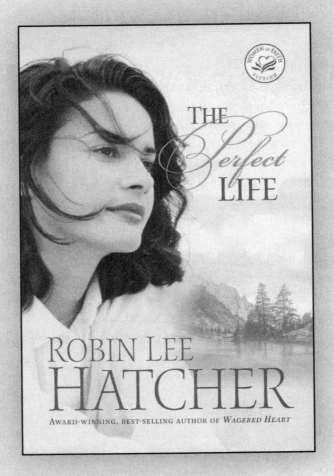

Available in print and e-book

THOMAS NELSON
Since 1798

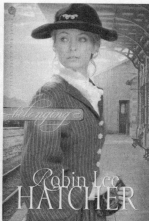

9781401687656-C

About the Author

Photo by J. L. Whitt Photography

Best-selling novelist Robin Lee Hatcher is known for her heart-warming and emotionally charged stories of faith, courage, and love. The winner of the Christy Award for Excellence in Christian Fiction, the RITA Award for Best Inspirational Romance, two RT Career Achievement Awards, and the RWA Lifetime Achievement Award, Robin is the author of over sixty novels.